SWIVEL

to Success

Bipolar Disorder in the Classroom:
A Teacher's Guide to Helping
Students Succeed

By Tracy Anglada

Please note that for ease of reading and writing, pronouns in the book are generally in the male gender but apply equally to females. No discrimination is intended by this usage. All brain pictures in this book are an artist's rendition and not a medical guide. Location of brain regions and structures are not meant to be exact but to simply give the reader a general guide.

ISBN 978-0-9817396-5-6

Published by BPChildren
P.O. Box 380075
Murdock, FL 33938

www.bpchildren.org

Dedicated to the many educators who make a difference in the lives of children with bipolar disorder every day.

Table of Contents

Acknowledgments

Many people have contributed to the collective knowledge that you will find in this book. First, and foremost, I would like to thank the researchers who work tirelessly at progressing our understanding of children with bipolar disorder. Your research becomes our basis of understanding and helping students with bipolar disorder. I would like to thank the many people who read this manuscript and offered suggestions. I would like to thank my editor, Andrew Randall, for his sharp eyes. I would also like to thank Dr. Donna Gilcher, Executive Director of The STARFISH Advocacy Association, whose leadership and knowledge in the area of educating children with bipolar disorder has been an inspiration.

Mostly, however, I would like to thank the children with bipolar disorder. Listening to you has taught me volumes. It is your courage to face this illness every day that inspires those who are brave enough to listen and care.

Introduction

This book is based upon a teacher workshop developed by BPChildren. BPChildren is an organization dedicated to helping young people and adults understand more about childhood bipolar disorder. Tracy Anglada is the founder and Executive Director of BPChildren. She is also the author of several other works on the topic of childhood bipolar disorder, including "Brandon and the Bipolar Bear: A Story for Children with Bipolar Disorder," "Turbo Max: A Story for Friends and Siblings of Children with Bipolar Disorder," and "Intense Minds: Through the Eyes of Young People with Bipolar Disorder." She is also co-author, with Dr. Sheryl Hakala, of "The Childhood Bipolar Disorder Answer Book: Practical Answers to the Top 300 Questions Parents Ask."

SWIVEL to Success is not designed to tell teachers how to do their jobs. You are trained professionals who are already skilled at teaching young minds. The purpose of this book is to present specialized knowledge about students with bipolar disorder. Without such knowledge, you are at a significant disadvantage when it comes to teaching students with bipolar disorder. Combining your skills with the information in this book can make a substantial impact on the success of your students with bipolar disorder.

If you would like to arrange to have a teacher workshop presented in your school, please email: tracy@bpchildren.org.

Chapter One

The Sharpie®

Imagine That ...

You hurry home from a long day with your students in the classroom and change into the clothes that you carefully selected and put out the night before. After quickly grabbing a bite to eat, you rush out the door with your bag in hand. You take a moment to breathe deeply and you chuckle at your own nervousness. Shaking your head, you think of the many night classes you have taken on the way to your degree. Why should this one presentation in the same lecture hall be so different? As you try to brush away the uncomfortable feeling that has settled in the pit of your stomach, one word comes to mind – HERO. This presentation isn't being given by just anyone. The presenter is your hero! Of course you're nervous and excited. It's a special night.

The 10 miles-per-hour speed limit on campus seems exceedingly slow today and the walk to the auditorium feels especially long. When you reach the lecture hall you see that it is already filling with people. As you wait in line to register and get your name badge, you wonder if these other people also appreciate the speaker today. In your bag you have personal copies of his work that you would like to have him autograph for you. You think about what you might say to your hero to convey just how much he has touched your life.

Suddenly you snap out of this preoccupation and realize that you are nearly to the front of the registration line. To your dismay, it is one of your instructors from a previous year who is handing out name tags. If the speaker you came to listen to is your hero, then this person is your antihero. You try to put the thoughts of your disagreements far from your mind. You don't want your experience today to be tainted in any way. Now, as you reach the table, you glance at the name tags being handed to the people in front of you. These are not ordinary name tags. They are descriptions. Could this be someone's idea of a joke? Amy smiles as she receives her tag, which reads "Model Student." Mark grimaces as he receives his tag, which reads "Frequently Tardy." Panic begins to set in. What possible descriptor would this instructor give to you - this instructor whose class you conveniently transferred out of after your ugly disagreement? With a quick flash of the Sharpie, your fate is sealed. You are to wear a tag which reads "Manipulator" in big bold letters.

You open your mouth to protest, as have several others before you, but it is to no avail. You are quickly ushered into the main hall and instructed to find your seat. Not only must you wear this name tag but you must sit with the others who have been labeled with the same description. You walk forward in shock. The tag feels heavy on your shirt. The stares of your colleagues make you feel as if you are wearing a scarlet letter across your chest instead of a simple name tag. Your heart sinks and you fight back the urge to simply run out of the auditorium. How can you face your peers, much less your hero? How can you ask for that autograph or be taken as a serious professional. As you sit next to your fellow "Manipulators" you see in them the same disheartened look. A quick glance around the room identifies the groups with positive qualities on their tags. They are chatting and laughing. The laughing is louder now and everyone begins looking and pointing at you. The laughing turns to a buzzing noise and suddenly you are jolted awake by your alarm clock! For a moment you are disoriented, and then a wave of relief descends upon you. It was a nightmare – just a terrible nightmare! The day has only begun.

The Nightmare

For some students this is a nightmare they don't get to wake up from. Every day they enter their classrooms weighed down with judgment. Every day they are thought of in terms of their worst traits. We are all guilty of classifying people to some extent, putting them in a category based on our impressions, using large brush strokes in describing all people with one condition or illness.

None of us can accurately be described in one word. Certainly none of us likes to be known for our weakest quality. This book will be discussing students who suffer with bipolar disorder. The first thing I want you to know is that "bipolar" is not an adjective to be applied to students. It is a medical condition shared by very different people. While the experiences they share and the challenges they face are similar, never forget that each student with bipolar disorder is a unique individual with both weaknesses and strengths. They are individuals who walk into your classroom hoping that you see more to them than a diagnosis. They can never be defined by their illness but they can be helped if you have knowledge of the challenges they face as a result of their medical condition.

What's in a Name?

In one of Shakespeare's most famous plays, Juliet asks the centuries old question, "What's in a name? That which we call a rose by any other name would smell as sweet." She saw past Romeo's family name to the man he was inside – a man she had fallen in love with. As you read this book, I ask that you see past the stigma and preconceived notions that may follow students with bipolar disorder. I ask that you set aside the Sharpie that may be poised to make a judgment. I ask that you read this material and then take a fresh look at your student using the "SWIVEL" method.

What does it mean to SWIVEL

The chart at the end of this chapter shows what each letter in the word SWIVEL represents. But more than an acronym, I would like you to think about the actual meaning of the word "swivel." One dictionary defines it this way – "To turn or pivot as if on a swivel." If you've ever taken a child to McDonald's or another fast-food restaurant then you know exactly what this means! That's because most kids run over and sit down in the chairs that go back and forth and annoyingly bang the table in the process. While kids are likely to sit in the chairs that swivel, adults are likely to pick the straight chair or bench. How do you think it changes a person's point of view to sit in the swivel chair and move back and forth versus sitting in a straight position? The truth is that when we sit in a fixed position our view is limited. We may find it difficult to change our position or to see things that aren't in our line of vision. But if we simply swivel, then we have a new view. A new view means new information and, in the case of children with bipolar disorder, new pathways to success.

Throughout this book, I'm going to be asking you to swivel either by direct invitation or by the type of information I present. I wish it were as easy to change our perspectives as sitting in those chairs at McDonald's – but it's not. Sometimes, our ideas or feelings have become very stiff and it can be really hard to break out of our current way of thinking. I don't expect you to master this immediately but each time you step out of a situation, turn, and think of it in a new way, it will become easier. Just the fact that you are reading this book may be a form of swiveling for you. When it becomes second nature to approach situations by swiveling your perspective then you will be pleasantly surprised with the results. But what if you are already a person who swivels simply by nature? What if you are the adult who runs to the swivel chairs? Then you already have an advantage. Hopefully this book will help you to continue coming up with new and fresh ideas to help your students with bipolar disorder. I would also encourage you to share your insights with others who may still be stuck in one position.

"SWIVEL"

Shift your perspective

Widen your view

Identify the underlying cause

Value the positives

Educate yourself

Learn how to help

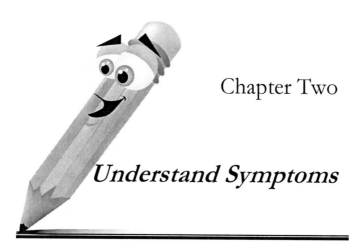

Chapter Two

Understand Symptoms

I Am

I am "odd and special."
I wonder when the paradise will get here.
I hear confusion in my life.
I see my life being ruined by others.
I want freedom.
I am "odd and special."

I pretend to be stable.
I feel the world's weight on my shoulders.
I touch my heart and it burns with red hot fire every day.
I worry that it won't go away.
I cry because I know it won't.
I am "odd and special."

(Written by a middle school student
with bipolar disorder.)

What is Bipolar Disorder?

Bipolar disorder is a highly heritable but treatable illness which affects the most important part of the body – the brain. Small changes on multiple genes responsible for the production of proteins and enzymes that control brain cell functioning and communication are currently the target of investigation by researchers studying the illness. More than 18 specific brain abnormalities have been found to occur more frequently in children with the illness. While researchers continue to search for the exact mechanism of illness, the results of the illness are well documented and can be devastating to those who suffer with it.

Extreme changes in mood, energy, thoughts and behavior send those who have this illness (and those around them) on a roller coaster ride of emotions. Moods cycle between the opposite extremes of mania and depression. Children with

✓ Mood
✓ Energy
✓ Thoughts
✓ Behavior

bipolar disorder tend to have very frequent cycles and also spend time in a mixed state where they are experiencing both mania and depression at the same time. Even during periods of wellness the illness takes its toll on those who suffer. Low frustration tolerance, faulty processing of facial expressions, faulty processing of the emotional meaning of language, and cognitive dysfunction in the areas of attention, information processing and memory are just some of the things these children must contend with even during times where mood symptoms seem to have abated. Let's learn more about this disorder and its symptoms.

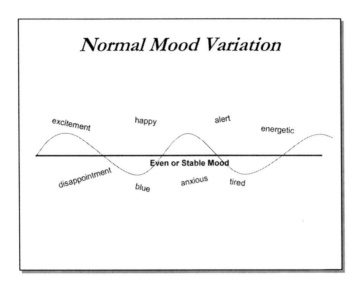

Normal Mood Variation

excitement — happy — alert — energetic

Even or Stable Mood

disappointment — blue — anxious — tired

What is normal?

Some people would argue that there is no such thing as normal because the world is full of very unique individuals with a wide range of personalities. A person's culture also dictates to one extent or another what is accepted as normal. Certainly, as a teacher you see a wide variety of personalities in the classroom. Every child has a natural degree of mood variation. In fact, it would be abnormal for a child not to experience a range of emotions from excitement to disappointment and so on. This is not what is being referred to in the diagnosis of bipolar disorder. It is also natural for a child to experience a stronger emotion for a period of time in response to certain life events. For instance, the loss of a pet may bring on sadness. This is normal. A party may cause a child to become very excited. This is normal. There is also natural variation from child to child due to personality differences. One child may be naturally outgoing and energetic. Another child may be more docile and quiet. None of these things would lead to a medical diagnosis of bipolar disorder.

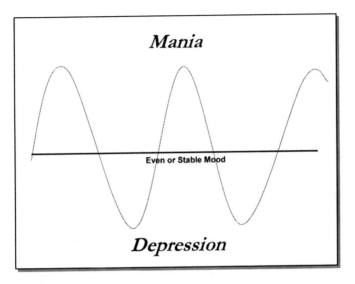

Opposite Extremes

To qualify for a diagnosis of bipolar disorder a child would experience the extremes in moods known as mania and depression. These are the two "poles" of bipolar disorder. These extremes go beyond what the average child experiences and can even cross over into very dangerous feelings and behaviors. These are not simply unique expressions of personality or a phase that will be outgrown. Mania and depression encompass a cluster of symptoms that interfere with the child's ability to function. Being able to identify and understand the symptoms of both mania and depression is essential to helping your student with bipolar disorder succeed in the classroom.

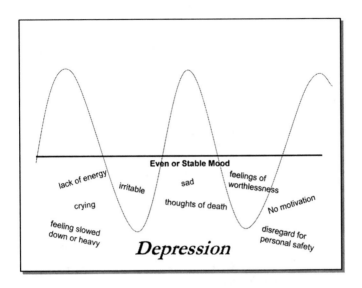

Even or Stable Mood

lack of energy

irritable

sad

feelings of worthlessness

crying

thoughts of death

No motivation

feeling slowed down or heavy

Depression

disregard for personal safety

Depression

Let's consider the depressive phase of bipolar disorder. Many children who begin to have symptoms of bipolar disorder will experience a depressive episode first. A child experiencing depression with a strong family history of bipolar disorder is at greater risk for developing bipolar disorder and should be watched for signs of "switching" into a manic state. Symptoms of a depressive state include:

- Decreased energy levels
- Excessive crying
- Lack of motivation
- Feelings of worthlessness
- Disregard for personal safety
- Sad or irritable mood
- Feels slowed down or heavy
- Thoughts of death or suicide

Beyond a List

There is something ironic about the fact that this list of symptoms for depression fits neatly on half a page in a book. It would be easy to quickly look over this list of symptoms – even read it seriously – and yet miss the gravity of these symptoms. Swiveling or changing your perspective to look at this from a different angle will help you understand and empathize with your student with bipolar disorder. Consider what these symptoms *feel* like to your student.

- *I just need to sleep. I'm so very tired. My brain is too slow to think. I don't have the energy to raise my hand. I have to rest my head on the desk. Please let me close my eyes just for a minute.*

- *Tears stream down my face. I can't keep myself from crying. I hate it when I cry in front of my classmates. Why can't I stop?*

- *I have so much work to do. What's the point anyway? When I finish there will just be more. Nothing seems worthwhile. I can't even get started.*

- *I deserve a bad grade. I deserve to fail. I am a failure. I'm not like the other kids. Something is wrong with me.*

- *I don't care if I get hurt. I'll just sit in the middle of the road. What will it matter if a car runs over me?*

- *I'm completely empty inside. I can't ever remember feeling happy. Everything annoys me. Just leave me alone.*

- *I feel like I'm walking through mud or quicksand. My arms and legs are very heavy. Everything is happening in slow motion.*

- *I want to close my eyes and go to sleep and never wake up. I want this nightmare to end. I pray to die ... please just let me die.*

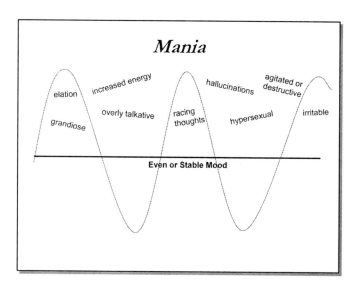

Mania

At the opposite end of the spectrum is mania. While many of the symptoms of mania are truly the opposite of depression, such as an increase in energy levels and elation, some children experience an irritable mood while in mania, which is a symptom that is also experienced with depression. Symptoms of a manic state include:

- Increased energy levels
- Elated or irritable mood
- Easily distracted
- Grandiose thinking
- Racing thoughts
- Overly talkative
- Agitated or Destructive
- Hypersexuality
- Hallucinations

A Closer Look

Just as it is difficult to get the full impact of the true nature of depression from a list of symptoms, so too one must take a closer look at how a child experiences mania to understand and empathize with the effect that these symptoms have on the child in the classroom. So take a minute to swivel and look closer at the symptoms of mania in children.

- *I feel like my skeleton will burst through my skin if I don't DO something ... anything. I have to move. I have to run. I can't sit in this chair.*

- *I feel pure joy. I will laugh, sing and shout at the top of my lungs. How can you sit quietly in class when it is the best day of your entire life?*

- *Someone walked in the door; the pencil sharpener is making noise; why is the person behind me tapping their pencil; the air conditioner is noisy. My turn to answer? What was the question?*

- *I deserve a better grade than this. I know more than the other kids. I'm too smart to be in school. I should be teaching this class.*

- *My head is spinning. I can't keep up with my own thoughts. They are coming too fast – like a buzzing in my brain. I can't focus on anything else.*

- *I know I'm talking too much but I can't stop. If only I could make them understand all the thoughts in my head. The words come out before I raise my hand.*

- *AARGH!! I'm mad at everything. I'm out of control. I can't stand it! I want to rip these papers up. I hate everything. Everyone else is making me mad.*

- *I can't stop thinking about sex. I feel aroused constantly. I blurt out the wrong thing. I dress like I feel.*

- *I can see a dead body in the teacher's closet. The door is open and I see it hanging there. How can I concentrate on my work with a dead body right there? I won't look at it. Is it still there? It's gone now. Where will it show up again? Did somebody move it? It's back again but on the floor of the closet now. Can you please close the closet door?*

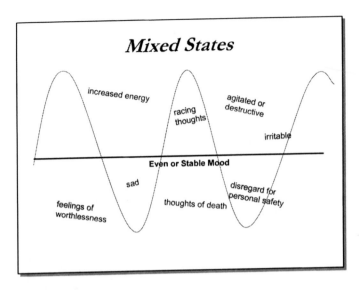

Mixed States

increased energy

racing thoughts

agitated or destructive

irritable

Even or Stable Mood

sad

disregard for personal safety

feelings of worthlessness

thoughts of death

Mixed States

As if it weren't bad enough for these children to bounce back and forth between the alternating extremes of emotions in mania and depression, they also experience what is known as a mixed state. This is basically the worst of both worlds. Take all of the negative emotions of depression and sprinkle in the agitation and energy of mania and you have a recipe for a mixed state – and for disaster! Suicide is a very real possibility in this state because the child may still be having thoughts of death but these are now combined with the energy to formulate and carry out a suicide plan. Swivel for a moment to see how this would feel:

- *Everything is wrong. The world is wrong. I hate myself. I want to die. I must do something. It can't stay this way. It's urgent. I can fix it now. I can end it all. I've figured it out. My problems will end ... forever.*

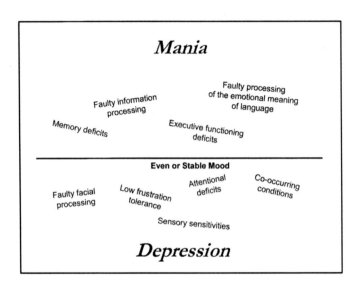

Mania

Faulty information processing

Faulty processing of the emotional meaning of language

Memory deficits

Executive functioning deficits

Even or Stable Mood

Faulty facial processing

Low frustration tolerance

Attentional deficits

Co-occurring conditions

Sensory sensitivities

Depression

More than Meets the Eye

Bipolar disorder is diagnosed when a child meets the criteria for having manic and depressive episodes. (Bipolar disorder is also classified by "type" depending on how symptoms present.) While that is all that is necessary for a diagnosis, the illness serves up much more. Rarely does bipolar disorder occur without additional challenges. The underlying mechanisms that cause the switching and extremes in moods also seem to have an effect on certain specific areas of cognition. Some of these deficits appear to be worse in an active mood state. Other deficits are constant even when the child's mood is stable. Here are some of the additional challenges facing children with bipolar disorder:

- Misinterpreting facial expressions (Neutral expressions interpreted as hostile)
- Misinterpreting the emotional meaning of language

- Information processing deficits
- Sensory sensitivities
- Low frustration tolerance
- Deficits in attention
- Deficits in executive functioning
- Co-occurring conditions

After this discussion of symptoms, you may have a better picture of everything these children have to face day in and day out. One of the few things children with bipolar disorder can count on is constantly changing moods. In later chapters, this book will discuss how these symptoms affect your student in the classroom and practical ways you can help your student be successful – but it all starts with having the full picture.

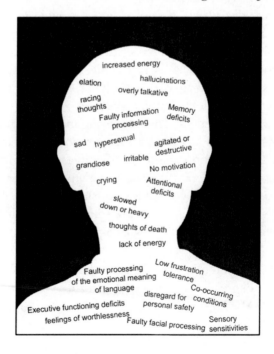

Don't Lose the Child

While it is vital for you to have the complete picture of symptoms when dealing with bipolar disorder in the classroom, it is equally important for you not to lose the child who exists underneath those symptoms. Bipolar disorder is this child's challenge. It's what he deals with every day, not who he is as a person. So along with the full picture of bipolar disorder make sure you swivel your point of view to see the gifts this child possesses. Your student with bipolar disorder may excel in artistic and creative areas. You may find that he is an "out-of-the-box" thinker whose unique view and imaginative thinking can bring much to a classroom environment. As you look closely you may find a youngster who has a strong desire to be included in a world that is difficult for him to survive in.

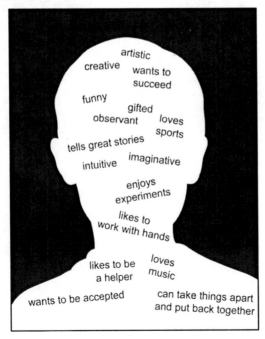

Behavior

Avoid Tunnel Vision

While some educators could fall into the trap of not seeing the child underneath the symptoms, others might fall into the trap of not seeing symptoms at all. This is a problem I like to call "tunnel vision." Tunnel vision is the polar opposite of swivel. It's seeing things in one set way. It's failing to adapt to the needs of the individual child. Tunnel vision keeps you clinging to ideas that probably work quite well for the majority of children but do little to help a child with bipolar disorder survive and thrive in your classroom. When an educator has tunnel vision he or she fails to understand the symptoms of bipolar disorder and approaches the child's difficulties as if they are all based in one thing – willful, deliberate behavior. This results in the idea that with coercion, discipline, consequences, etc., the child will "straighten up" and that his behaviors will disappear. While children with bipolar disorder are still children and do have normal behaviors which respond to discipline, their symptoms are not part of this equation. While behavioral techniques will always have their place, there is no discipline or consequence that will stop a child from having an hallucination or racing thoughts or feelings of worthlessness.

A more successful approach will be to help students to deal with their illness. This happens in stages from identifying and reporting symptoms all the way to successfully managing strong emotions in ways that do not hinder the learning environment. Such an approach will foster an atmosphere of trust in which the student feels comfortable reaching out to you for help when needed. This is especially vital when a child is having suicidal thoughts. One study revealed that up to a third of children with bipolar disorder attempt suicide. Children should always be taken seriously when expressing thoughts or feelings of taking their own lives. They should not be punished or rebuked for entrusting their feelings to an adult.

Avoiding tunnel vision and fully understanding both the child and the symptoms of the illness will set the basis for a successful classroom. To that end, we are going to take a journey through the brain of children with bipolar disorder to get a better understanding of their impairments.

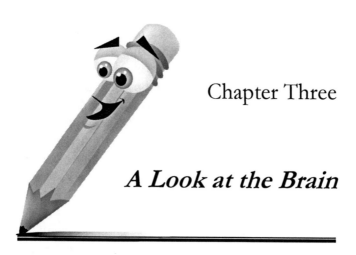

Chapter Three

A Look at the Brain

The Amazing Brain

As an educator you are no doubt constantly amazed at the process of learning. Watching a student learn a new skill or take a big step in academics is a rewarding experience. All of this is possible because of the amazing brain. Man has barely scratched the surface in understanding this organ but one thing is for certain – every function of the body is interrelated to the brain. From a blink of the eye to the beat of a heart everything can be traced back to this amazing organ. So what happens when something goes wrong in the brain? There are many illnesses that strike the brain. Seizures, tumors and illnesses such as Alzheimer's and Parkinson's all wreak havoc on the brain and subsequently upon the person. Bipolar disorder also has an effect on the brain.

While researchers are still learning a great deal about the brain abnormalities associated with childhood bipolar disorder, it's very enlightening to examine what is known. It is also very helpful as we swivel our perspective. First, however, it should be noted that none of the following abnormalities are used for diagnosing bipolar disorder but they are abnormalities found at a higher rate among children with bipolar disorder than among the general population of healthy children. Not every child with bipolar disorder will have each of these impairments and the degree to which each child is affected varies greatly. The brain scans used for research purposes are highly specialized and not as yet part of routine care when treating children with bipolar disorder.

Brain abnormalities fall into one of three basic categories – structural, functional and chemical. A structural abnormality means that the physical size or makeup of the area of the brain is altered. A functional abnormality means that the area of the brain may be of the correct size and makeup but is not functioning properly. It may be overactive, underactive or simply active at the wrong time or in response to the wrong thing. A chemical abnormality means that the chemical messengers in the area of the brain are off balance. At times an area of the brain will be altered in all three of these ways. The brain abnormalities associated with bipolar disorder fall into all three of these categories.

✓ Structural

✓ Functional

✓ Chemical

As you read this section it may be helpful to refer to the chart on the next page. It will help in defining some of the common terms used when talking about brain regions and functioning.

English Please

Anterior – comes from the Latin word 'ante,' meaning before. It refers to the position of something being closest to the head or front.

Cingulate – comes from the Latin word 'cingere,' meaning girdle or belt. It refers to a particular zone or 'belt like' area of the brain.

Cortex – a Latin word meaning 'bark,' 'shell' or 'husk.' When used in relation to the brain it means the outer region.

Gyrus – comes from the Greek word 'gyro,' meaning circle. It refers to the crest or rounded ridge of a fold in the brain.

Gray Matter – made up of cell bodies and responsible for information processing.

Lobe (or Lobule) – a well-defined portion or division. (Lobule – subdivision of a lobe.)

Superior – situated above or upward.

White Matter – made up of nerve fibers which have a protective coating that is white in appearance. White matter helps different parts of the brain communicate with each other and the rest of the body.

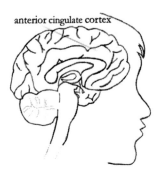

anterior cingulate cortex

Anterior Cingulate Cortex (ACC)

Although you may not know too much about the anterior cingulate cortex, it is likely that you are already familiar with some of the negative effects when this area of the brain is impaired.

That's because this is the same area of the brain that is responsible for impaired judgment when someone drinks too much alcohol.

The ACC is a front outer region of the brain. It is thought to be involved in decision making, cognitive functioning, such as memory and attention, perceptual awareness and emotion. Researchers have found all three abnormality types (structural, functional and chemical) in this part of the brain in children with bipolar disorder.

- **Changes in gray matter** – Gray matter is vital to information processing. Studies indicate abnormal changes in the gray matter over time.

- **Lower glutamine levels** – Glutamine is an energy source for the brain. It is a building block to neurotransmitters such as GABA and also helps detoxify cells. Reduced levels of glutamine can be a sign of stress.

- **Decreased response to emotional faces** – the ACC should "activate" or work to process emotional faces. This response is decreased in children with bipolar disorder. Instead of using this cognitive area of the brain you will see later on that a highly emotional area of the brain is overactive during this task.

- **Increased DNA fragmentation** in some neurons – DNA fragmentation is a sign of cellular death. While cellular death is a normal part of the life cycle of a cell this increased amount of fragmentation is more than would be expected and may be an indication of increased neuronal loss in children with bipolar disorder.

Cingulate Gyrus

Children with bipolar disorder frequently have difficulty with strong emotional responses, correctly processing stimuli, and with aggression. It comes as no surprise then that there is an abnormality in the cingulate gyrus. This area of the brain has been linked to aggression and to the emotional response that a person has to stimuli. It is also thought that the anterior cingulate gyrus helps regulate the activities of the frontal cortex. In children with bipolar disorder this area of the brain has a smaller volume of gray matter in the left anterior (or front) portion. Remember, gray matter is vital to information processing. If the brain cannot correctly process information then the conclusion it reaches and the reaction that follows is faulty as well.

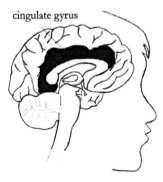

cingulate gyrus

Frontal Lobe

If you were to place your hand on the top forward part of your head, you would be directly over your frontal lobe. This area of the brain is involved in the higher thinking skills. It is where reasoning, judgment, impulse control, problem solving, attention, socializing and language all come together. It is also the location of white matter lesions in childhood bipolar disorder which progressively get worse over time with repeated episodes. White matter lesions are actually a fairly common brain abnormality. They are especially common among elderly patients and are associated with a greater degree of impairment in patients with dementia. White matter protects nerve fibers and plays an important role in the brain's ability to communicate with itself and the rest of the body. When part of this white protective coating is missing this is referred to as a lesion.

Prefrontal Cortex

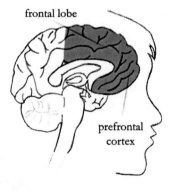
frontal lobe

prefrontal cortex

If you slide your hand from the top forward part of your head down onto your forehead you are now over the area of the frontal lobe known as the prefrontal cortex. This part of the brain is thought to be involved in planning, sequencing, working memory, judgment, and social control. The prefrontal cortex is an area that has all three brain abnormality types – structural, functional, and chemical.

- **Lower ratios of N-acetylaspartate (NAA)/ creatine** – lower ratios of these amino acids are also found in epilepsy, stroke and other disorders of the brain. It is thought to represent neuronal loss or damage.
- **Abnormal amounts of gray matter** – being decreased in the left and increased ventrally (lower surface).
- **Abnormal activation** – part of the function of the prefrontal cortex is to activate in response to negative stimuli. This helps the person inhibit actions and control emotional responses. However, there is reduced activation of this higher thinking area of the brain combined with an overaction of reactive and emotional parts of the brain.

Temporal Lobe

If you place each of your hands over your ears on either side of your head, you are covering not only your ears but, below the surface, you are covering the temporal lobes of your brain. As one might suspect by the location of the temporal lobes, they are home to the area of the brain responsible for processing sound information and for higher level auditory processing such as speech. But the temporal lobes do much more, including processing very complex visual stimuli such as faces. They are also involved in forming memories and understanding emotional context.

We will be discussing specific components of the temporal lobes but overall the structure of this area of the brain is abnormal. It has a reduced average volume and increased gray matter on the left side.

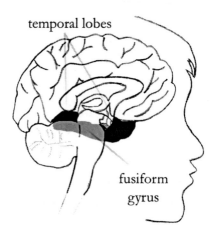

temporal lobes

fusiform
gyrus

Fusiform Gyrus

Can you sometimes tell just by a student's facial expression that he is confused, or perhaps you can see when he grasps a new concept? Can you detect by your student's face when he is happy or sad or angry? You probably haven't given it much thought as this is a very automatic process for most people. The fusiform gyrus is one of the areas of the brain involved in this task. When you identify the emotional meaning of expressions you don't think about which part of the brain is doing the job or the balance in this process that allows you to do this properly. But these tasks are not so easy for children with bipolar disorder. We have already seen that the prefrontal cortex is underactive in this task. Now as we move to the fusiform gyrus we see that it is overactive during this task. The result is that children with bipolar disorder perceive neutral faces as hostile. This part of the brain also has increased gray matter – remember, gray matter is involved in information processing. The fusiform gyrus is also an area with abnormal activation in children with autism.

Right and Left Amygdala

Another part of the brain that resides in the temporal lobe is the amygdala – and it too plays a role in facial processing. This part of the brain is the size and shape of an almond. The amygdala is primarily known for its fight or flight emotional response. This is the part of the brain that instinctively takes over when a threat is perceived. The amygdala has three documented abnormalities in children with bipolar disorder.

- **Reduced gray matter**
- **Abnormal development of the left Amygdala** – this is an abnormality that worsens over time as this part of the brain doesn't develop as expected.
- **Increased activation to emotional faces** – this part of the brain appears to be responsible for the emotional response to faces that are incorrectly viewed as hostile and threatening.

Hippocampus

As we arrive at the hippocampus, known for formation of memories and associations, we have our first and only known gender-related difference in the brains of children with bipolar disorder. There is a reduction in the volume of this area most notable in girls with bipolar disorder.

Superior Temporal Gyrus

The superior temporal gyrus – yet another area in the temporal lobe – relates to insight, music and processing speech. There is a reduction in white matter in this area of the brain. Remember that white matter is especially important for the brain to communicate with itself and other parts of the body. Additionally, this area of the brain has a smaller total volume on the left side.

Time Out

Congratulations on making it this far. While some people are naturally intrigued by this type of discussion, I know that others are poised right now to flip the pages to the next chapter. If you are one who has had enough brain talk, I would like to entice you to hang in for the rest of the discussion by telling you about my favorite brain abnormality. Sound a bit strange? I know. But read on to find out about this very fascinating brain abnormality and then I promise that I will move you quickly through the final brain abnormalities and on into the classroom. Deal?

The Fascinating Septum Pellucidum

The septum pellucidum is a triangular shaped membrane that lies deep within the brain and separates the right and left hemispheres of the brain. It is actually made up of two distinct membranes. When a baby is born these membranes are separate, having a small space between them. As a baby grows the two membranes fuse together to form one. Why should we care about this membrane? It is thought to be a relay within the limbic system. The limbic system is an emotional circuitry of sorts. It's made up of the parts of the brain that are involved in emotion, motivation and the emotional association of memory. Several of the previous brain areas that we talked about are included in the limbic system.

The fascinating thing about these two small membranes is that by the time an infant is 3-6 months old these membranes fuse together as one ... or at least they are supposed to. When these membranes don't fuse together there is a cavity left between them. A tiny cavity may not be considered abnormal but in adults who had a childhood onset of bipolar disorder this cavity was not only present at a higher rate but also enlarged. This was different from adults who had onset of bipolar disorder later in life. Whenever there is an enlarged cavity between these two membranes it's called "cavum septi pellucidi" and it is strongly correlated to neuropsychiatric disorders including bipolar disorder.

septum pellucidum

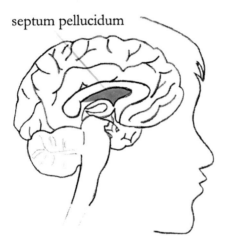

So what's the big deal? The big deal is that this abnormality always begins in infancy. I am not suggesting that doctors can diagnose or treat an infant for bipolar disorder. But long before the child grows and shows the full range of symptoms that will lead to the diagnosis of bipolar disorder, we are still parenting and teaching this child who may already be experiencing an abnormality deep within the brain – an abnormality that began before he could even walk or talk.

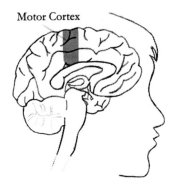

Motor Cortex

Motor Cortex

The motor cortex runs like a headband over the two sides of the brain and is responsible for all voluntary movements of the body. Prior to sending out the signals to initiate movement this part of the brain receives messages from many other parts of the brain including communication about the intention or goal of the movement, memory of past movement, and the body's position or orientation in space. Fine motor control takes up more space along this strip. Damage to the motor cortex can result in loss of mobility such as in the case of a stroke. Children with bipolar disorder have higher rates of increased gray matter in the motor cortex.

Orbitofrontal Cortex

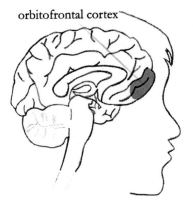

orbitofrontal cortex

This small area directly behind the eyes has been linked to motivation, mood, responsibility and addiction. Abnormal gray matter volumes have been found in this area of the brain in children with bipolar disorder.

Striatum

For the next few brain abnormalities we return to the temporal lobes located on either side of the head behind the ears. The Striatum is part of the Basal Ganglia System which is found in both hemispheres of the brain and is involved in starting, controlling, modifying and inhibiting movement on a minute-by-minute basis. It works in concert with the Thalamus and the Cerebral Cortex. Together these form circuits that play a role in reinforcing wanted behavior, learning by habit, suppressing unwanted behavior, and changing attention sets. The Striatum is the largest collection of nuclei within the Basal Ganglia. This area has abnormal volume changes that progress with age in children with bipolar disorder.

Right Nucleus Accumbens

This area of the brain is a collection of neurons within the striatum which helps to modulate the flow of information to other areas of the brain. It plays a part in modulating desire, inhibition and satisfaction. The Right Nucleus Accumbens has a larger volume which is especially pronounced in prepuberty. This area of the brain is also implicated in obsessive-compulsive disorder and anxiety disorders.

Putamen

The Putamen is another part of the Striatum. Along with motor control it plays a role in sensory motor integration. Researchers have found that children with bipolar disorder are more likely to have this area of the brain enlarged and with increased activation.

Thalamus

The thalamus is a bullet-shaped collection of nerve cells that is situated very near the middle of the brain. The thalamus is in both the right and left hemispheres of the brain and is connected in the middle. It plays

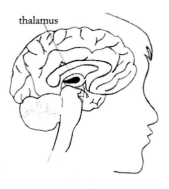

an important role in processing sensory information and translating that information for the cortex. It is also involved in the sleep/wake cycle and in regulating arousal levels. In children with bipolar disorder this area of the brain is found to be overactive.

Superior Parietal Lobule

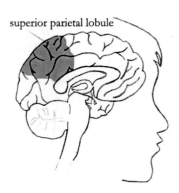

Spatial orientation is the body's ability to know where it is relative to the space around it. It is what we use when we turn a somersault or simply walk down the hallway. The Superior Parietal Lobule is an area of the brain heavily involved with spatial orientation. A decrease in gray matter in this area of the brain has been noted in children with bipolar disorder.

Whole Brain

Last but not least, when we examine the brain as a whole, children with bipolar disorder are more likely to have a smaller total volume, which may be due to the cumulative effect of the various brain abnormalities listed above.

Ending our Journey

This ends our examination of the many brain areas impacted in children with bipolar disorder. Researchers continue to peer into the brain and, as they do so, increase our understanding of this illness. Next we will swivel into the classroom; but before we do, here is a brief review of the various functions of the brain areas which have been found to have abnormalities in childhood bipolar disorder.

- Decision making
- Emotion/Mood
- Response to stimuli
- Aggression
- Impulse control
- Planning
- Reasoning /Judgment
- Desire/Satisfaction
- Attention
- Problem solving
- Language
- Socializing
- Inhibition
- Facial processing
- Memories
- Associations
- Motor movement
- Spatial orientation
- Motivation
- Responsibility
- Addiction
- Planning
- Sequencing
- Social control
- Sensory motor integration
- Perception

Chapter Four

Effects in the Classroom

How does bipolar disorder impact school?

There are four primary ways in which bipolar disorder affects the functioning of a child in the classroom: active symptoms, deficits in cognition, co-occurring conditions and medication side effects. The degree to which the illness impacts an individual will vary from student to student and can also vary from year to year, month to month and day to day due to the cyclical nature of the illness.

> ✓ Active Symptoms
> ✓ Deficits in Cognition
> ✓ Co-occurring Conditions
> ✓ Medication Side Effects

1. Active Symptoms

The most obvious and direct way in which bipolar disorder affects a child in the classroom is through active symptoms. The more symptomatic the student the greater impact this will have on functioning in the classroom. Whether your student is experiencing depression, mania or a mixed state the results can be equally detrimental to learning and functioning in the classroom. We've already learned about the symptoms of each of these phases of the illness and how this feels to the child but let's take that a step further and see how each symptom in the various mood states can have an impact on the student's school day.

Depression

- **Decreased energy levels** – this symptom makes it difficult for your student to make it to school on time. He may sleep 12 or more hours and still feel wiped out with no energy. If he can make it to school, he may sleep through a good portion of class. Even if he stays awake physically, his mind is still sleepy. *Example: Michael drags into class with his usual tardy slip in hand. He plops down in his chair and immediately puts his head on the desk. You ask him to take out his book and follow along. He pulls out his book slowly and turns to the right page. After you finish writing the notes on the chalkboard you turn to find that Michael is now using his book as a pillow.*

- **Excessive crying** – when a student with bipolar disorder cries in the classroom it creates several problems for a successful learning environment that can linger long after the incident is over. It generally creates a disturbance of some sort but it also creates a social taboo, especially during the middle school years. Many students who are experiencing this symptom live in fear that they will break down in the classroom. *Example: Emma has seemed withdrawn and emotionally delicate for the past week. She has come to your desk on several occasions with teary eyes and asked to be excused to go to the bathroom. Today she breaks down in tears for no apparent reason. Your other students are whispering and pretending not to look at her. She runs out of class and down to the counselor's office. The next day you hear that she is refusing to come to school.*

- **Lack of motivation** – without motivation it is difficult to inspire students to reach their full potential. Learning is an active process and requires participation on the part of the student. When depression robs a student of motivation, then many of the typical methods of teaching no longer work well. *Example: Christopher hasn't turned in a homework assignment all week. He seems listless and uninterested. You warn him that he will not be able to participate in the school rally on Friday unless he turns in all his assignments. His reply of "Whatever!" doesn't give you any hope that the work will get done.*

- **Feelings of worthlessness** – this symptom comes through in the classroom setting in several ways. If a student has little sense of self worth then they see little value in their contributions to the class. They look on commendation and rewards as undeserved and wasted. They internalize constructive criticism and twist it to mean they are not doing anything right. In the end these feelings may lead them to give up entirely. *Example: Abigail is stuck on a math problem. When you try to help her work through it she says she can't do anything right. When you point out her good grade in another subject she rolls her eyes and grunts. She doesn't seem to be listening or willing to try to work through the problem.*

- **Disregard for personal safety** – this is a dangerous symptom of depression because it involves risky behaviors that can put your student in harm's way. While many times this occurs outside of the classroom it can also happen at school. *Example: William is playing team sports during gym class. He seems to find all the dangerous spots on the court and has been knocked down several times. Now, as the team is supposed to be running laps, they stop and point at the bleachers. When you look up you see William on top of the railing of the highest bleacher attempting a dangerous high-wire act.*

- **Sad or irritable** – a persistently sad mood in the classroom can be heartbreaking to observe. While some learning may take place the material presented seems to engulf and overwhelm the student and take on some of his own sadness. *Example: Sophia sits in your history class with a hollow, empty look. After the lecture you ask if there is anything bothering her. Sophia says, "Don't you think it's sad that all the people we are studying are dead?" As you try to explain how their accomplishments continue to live on and influence the present world, Sophia seems to have slipped back into her own private thoughts.*

- **Feels slowed down or heavy** – this symptom goes hand-in-hand with reduced energy but refers more to a specific feeling of heaviness. When a student is experiencing this, then any additional pressure or task is very overwhelming. *Example: Robert has been working slowly all morning on the same worksheet. He breaks the tip of his pencil and walks to the sharpener as though he has weights attached to both legs. As he slowly sharpens the pencil, you wonder if he is turning the lever fast enough to actually sharpen anything. Robert makes the laborious trip back to his seat. When he breaks his pencil a second time, you give him two extra ones because you can't stand to watch the slow walk to the sharpener again.*

- **Thoughts of death or suicide** – this is a very scary symptom and can spill over into the classroom in several ways. Persistent thoughts of death can overtake your student's thinking to the point that he is unable to concentrate on the work at hand or feels that the work is pointless. There have been cases in schools where students actually take sharp objects and make suicide attempts in the bathroom. *Example: Beth has been thinking about her funeral and death. You notice that she gives a fellow classmate her calculator and she gives her necklace to another student. She seems preoccupied in class writing a note in her notebook instead of listening. She doesn't write down the assignment. The next day her seat is empty and it isn't until later that you learn she has been hospitalized after a suicide attempt.*

Mania

- **Increased energy levels** – high energy levels on the playground is one thing but in the classroom it can hinder learning. Your student may be fidgety, pacing, bursting at the seams. The physical movement that comes with this symptom can be disruptive to learning. It can also lead to a child running off campus or out of the classroom. In high school, a student may take on an excessive amount of projects, clubs and activities to occupy this energy. Unfortunately, when the inevitable crash comes, these turn into perceived failures. *Example: Johnny is supposed to be sitting quietly in circle reading time but instead gets up and runs around the circle. Upon being reprimanded, he sits down then lies back on the floor and moves his legs up and down.*

- **Elated or irritable** – a child experiencing elation may start laughing uncontrollably in class and not be able to stop. Combined with increased energy, the elated student may be hopping, jumping or skipping about the classroom. An irritable mood will create more than just a cranky student. It can lead to arguments with the fellow classmates and the teacher. *Example: Susan is trying to work as a team with her partner Alicia but Alicia is irritable and argumentative. The two are unable to come to an agreement on even minor aspects of the project. Alicia feels that it is all Susan's fault. When you try to point out ways to work together, Alicia becomes angry with you and says that you are causing the whole problem.*

- **Easily distracted** – imagine trying to work on schoolwork when your senses seem to be stuck in overdrive. A student in mania may pick up on every noise and sensation in the classroom. Every shuffle of the papers or humming of the fluorescent lights takes the focus of attention off the task at hand. *Example: Joel is supposed to complete a math sheet with 20 problems on it before lunch. Joel makes an attempt to start the problems but has to restart every few minutes after something distracts him. By lunchtime the worksheet is not even a third of the way completed.*

- **Grandiose thinking** – this symptom looks very disrespectful in the classroom. If the child is feeling grandiose then he has a feeling of superiority over everyone else in the classroom, including you as the teacher. This may cause him to feel above the current work in the classroom. After all, why should he do schoolwork if he is already smarter than the teacher? This state of mind, which is part of mania, is very hard for others to understand because it can be offensive; nevertheless, it is merely a reflection of the student's current mood state. *Example: Mary loudly complains when she is given her assignment. She says it's for babies and insulting. She refuses to even look at it. She interrupts your lecture and proceeds to explain why you and your way of teaching are wrong.*

- **Racing thoughts** – this symptom has definite effects in the classroom but is more of a private experience since it effects a student's thinking. When a child has many thoughts swirling in his head at once and his mind is racing from one topic to the next at top speed, whatever information that you were trying to share with the class is not breaking through that barrier. *Example: Mark receives his assignment but he alternates between staring at the paper and turning his gaze to every tiny disturbance in the room. When you prompt him to begin he says he doesn't know what* to do despite the fact that you just went through the *instructions*.

- **Overly talkative** – racing thoughts often spill out with this next symptom of over-talkativeness. The student not only talks too much but is frequently way too loud while talking and will find it quite difficult to refrain from talking even when it is inappropriate timing. *Example: Kimberly has shouted out every answer all morning and now, at free time, hers is the only voice you hear clearly above the rest. When her classmates tire of her endless talk she comes over to you and tells you stories. You have trouble getting her to stop.*

- **Agitated or Destructive** – a student having this symptom can be quite unpleasant. Because he is already internally agitated any outside stressor can send him over the edge. *Example: Raymond has a scowl on his face. When given an assignment he presses so hard on the paper that his pencil snaps. He wads up his assignment. When asked to get out a new piece of paper, he shoves his book off his desk and onto the floor.*

- **Hypersexuality** – a student experiencing hypersexuality is driven by a strong sexual urge which makes paying attention to anything else difficult. The student may draw inappropriate pictures or say inappropriate things to other classmates. *Example: Two classmates come running down the hallway to tell you that Jill just went into the bathroom and pulled down her pants in front of everyone and asked if they wanted to touch her.*

- **Hallucinations** – this is another symptom that may or may not be readily noticeable by you as the teacher but has a very large impact on the classroom experience. Children do not always share when they are having a hallucination. Hallucinations can come in the form of auditory, visual or tactile experiences. In other words your student may see, hear or feel things that aren't there. Sometimes they are aware that the hallucination is not real but it still leaves an imprint on their mind. Hallucinations can be exacerbated by stress. *Example: Ethan begins to take his timed math test. He sees ants crawling on his paper. They feel like they are crawling up his arm. Ethan pushes his paper to the floor. The teacher picks it up as the timer buzzes and writes a zero in red ink. As she puts the paper back on Ethan's desk he sees the red ink turn to blood and drip down. He wads it up and throws it away never once telling the teacher or other students what he saw.*

Cycling

The tricky thing about how active symptoms impact a student in your classroom is that you don't just get to pick one symptom and learn how to deal with it. Rather, both in mania and in depression, the student will exhibit several of the symptoms at the same time. While some children will have one prominent mood state for a period that may last for weeks or months, many children with bipolar disorder will rapidly bounce between the mood states. So at morning announcements you may have a child in mania or depression but by recess that may have switched to the opposite mood state. Additionally, the mixed state throws in symptoms at both ends of the spectrum.

Example: Tanya bounces into the classroom in time for morning announcements. She sharpens every pencil she owns and takes out three or four worksheets and a coloring project. Her mother has told you that she has been averaging only four hours of sleep at night and she hasn't been able to shut her mind off. You have difficulty settling her in and she pays no attention to classroom instruction because she is "working on an important assignment." Her incessant talking and pacing between her project and various areas of the room are a distraction to the other students. At lunch she is still buzzing but you notice a change in her demeanor. While she is still running at full speed, she has become irritable and argumentative with classmates. At recess she disappears from your sight as you help another student. You find her hiding behind some play equipment crying and attempting to scrape at her skin with a stick she has found on the playground. She is still talking rapidly but now it is about wanting to die. When you ask her to go with another teacher to the nurse's office she tries to run off the campus grounds.

2. Deficits in Cognition

The second way that bipolar disorder affects a student in the classroom is through deficits in the area of cognition. After examining the abnormalities in various brain regions associated with childhood bipolar disorder, it should not be surprising that cognition is impacted. You may find that an individual student has more difficulty with cognition during an active mood state but even when stable these deficits can remain.

Deficits may be most notable in the areas of executive functioning. The child's ability to plan, organize, break a project down into smaller steps, and logically execute these steps may be lacking. Additionally, memory and attention can remain impaired. Learning things by rote memorization may be difficult. You may also notice general glitches in the way your student processes information. Additionally, sensory sensitivities and tactile defensiveness may be present both during active mood states and during stability. Misinterpretation of the emotional meaning of words as well as facial expressions are known characteristics of the illness that can worsen in some mood states but also remain during stability. The advantage of a child dealing with these issues in a stable mood is that he will have more emotional resources available to him to deal with these extra challenges.

It should be noted that along with active symptoms, the deficits found in processing facial expression and the emotional meaning of language also have a direct impact on the student's social skills. This can be a vicious cycle because lack of friends and feeling isolated in the social setting can feed into depressive moods.

3. Co-occurring Conditions

As if bipolar disorder alone is not enough of a challenge for your student to deal with, there are many co-occurring conditions that frequently go hand-in-hand with bipolar disorder. Attention-deficit hyperactivity disorder, learning disorders, oppositional defiant disorder and anxiety disorders (such as obsessive-compulsive disorder, panic disorder, post-traumatic stress disorder and generalized anxiety disorder) are among the most common conditions to occur along with bipolar disorder. These will have a separate impact in the classroom and can affect how symptoms of the illness are displayed. While the rates of occurrence are still being researched and figures will vary depending on the research study cited, the chart on the next page outlines some of the more common co-occurring conditions and the estimated rates of their existence with bipolar disorder.

Rates of Co-occurring Conditions	
Co-occurring Condition	*How often does it occur with childhood bipolar?*
Attention-Deficit Hyperactivity Disorder (ADHD)	Up to 90% in childhood onset and up to 40% in teenage onset.
Anxiety Disorders (includes OCD)	Up to 56%
Asperger's Disorder	Up to 11% Others have more severe forms of developmental disorders, including autism.
Conduct Disorders	Up to 37%
Oppositional Defiant Disorder	Up to 75%
Tourette's Syndrome	Tourette's patients are 4 times more likely to also have bipolar disorder.
Learning Disabilities	Reports indicate that up to 50% have disorders of written expression. Other learning disabilities may also be found.
Substance Abuse	Up to 40%

4. Medication Side Effects

Treating children with bipolar disorder typically involves medication. We will be discussing how treatment can help your student and your role in this process in the next chapter but it must be noted here that medication can also have some negative effects in the classroom environment. Finding the right medication at the right dosage or in combination with other medications can be quite tricky and takes some trial and error. Treating co-occurring conditions can be even more troublesome since treatment for one condition may exacerbate symptoms of bipolar disorder. Even once a student has found a very good medication regime which controls his symptoms it is not uncommon to have frequent medication adjustments to maintain stability.

When a medication trial is first started the student may especially be affected by side effects that later subside. Other side effects will persist and must be considered against the benefit that is being received from the medication. Weight gain is an especially common side effect of many of the medications. This particular side effect can cause a social stigma, especially in the teen years. Here are some of the side effects that may affect your student in the classroom environment:

- sleepiness
- insomnia
- hand tremor
- stomach ache/headache
- cognitive dulling
- vision disturbance
- frequent urination

- thirst/dry mouth
- hunger
- constipation/diarrhea
- dizziness
- weight gain

Individual Students

Ironically, you may actually have a student diagnosed with bipolar disorder who is your absolute top performer and has few outward symptoms for the majority of the school year. How and why can this happen with the level of effects outlined in this chapter? Many factors come together to determine the individual functioning of each student. Here are the primary factors involved in an individual student's functioning:

- **Age of onset** – Earlier onset means fewer milestones met while healthy and generally a more severe illness course.

- **Severity of illness** – Some children have a more severe form of the illness while others have a milder presentation. More time spent in active mood states means more interference with development.

- **Presence of co-occurring conditions** – The more co-occurring conditions that are present the more symptoms are present and the more complicated treatment becomes. Treatment becomes especially complex when the co-occurring condition is substance abuse.

- **Response to treatment** – Some children respond quickly and well to treatment. Others have multiple negative reactions to medications or only partial response to treatment. It can take years for some children to stabilize on medications. Others only stabilize for very short periods of time before relapsing.

- **Medication Compliance** – The success of any treatment regime is dependent on compliance. Forgotten medication doses, lapse in medication due to financial constraints, and deliberate medication avoidance can all jeopardize a child's treatment success.

- **Skill of treating physician** – The skill and knowledge level of the treating physician can affect outcome. If a physician does not identify the correct diagnosis, then the child may spend precious months or years receiving the wrong treatment with little improvement or even a worsening of symptoms.

- **Support level at school** – Appropriate support at school can make a huge difference in the functioning of a student with bipolar disorder. We have dedicated the latter chapters of this book to discussing that support.

- **Support level at home** – There are some families who refuse to get help for a child who is clearly suffering with symptoms of a psychiatric disorder due to perceived stigma, financial distress, or simply lack of education. This will have a big impact on the student.

Quick Review: Problems in the classroom.

- Initiating tasks

- Maintaining attention

- Organizing materials

- Planning ahead

- Memorizing facts

- Interacting socially

- Remaining seated

- Sensory processing

- Completing assignments

- Frequent absenteeism

- Crying spells

- Sleeping in class

- Angry outbursts

- Loud talking

- Panic attacks

- Frequent trips to the nurse's office

Chapter Five

Treatment

Your Role in Wellness

The good news is that there is treatment to help children who suffer with bipolar disorder. For a treatment plan to be effective it must support the child in three main areas – medical treatment, family support and school support. A comprehensive approach gives the child the best chance to move toward stability and wellness which in turn will help him be successful in school. As a teacher, you will have a large role in supporting this child in school but you also play secondary roles in the areas of medical treatment and family support. How so?

Medical Treatment

The parent is the primary person responsible for coordinating a child's care and the physician is responsible for evaluating, diagnosing and treating. How then can a teacher help in the medical aspect of treatment? Students spend a large portion of their day in the classroom. Many treatment decisions are made on the basis of how effectively medications are eliminating symptoms and if these medications are resulting in excessive side effects. A child's teacher becomes an important partner in reporting symptoms and observations as to the child's functioning throughout the day. This feedback can be invaluable to the parent as treatment decisions are made. A parent may ask you to complete a simple mood chart throughout the day and send it home in the child's folder. This is a quick and easy way to keep the channel of communication open and for mood symptoms to be recorded. A simple mood chart can be found in Appendix A of this book or online at www.bpchildren.org/Charting.html. This reporting may lead to a medication adjustment that makes all the difference for your student. Of course balance and caution are necessary when dealing with sensitive and private medical information. This would not be the topic of lunchroom discussion and a parent may not want you to have direct access to the child's physician due to privacy concerns.

Common Medications

There are FDA approved medications to treat children and adolescents with bipolar disorder. Additionally, there are other medications approved in adults that are also sometimes used to treat children. Here is an overview of the more commonly used medications that your student may take.

1. **Lithium** – Lithium is actually a naturally occurring mineral. It has the longest track record in treating patients with bipolar disorder but comes with some drawbacks that you need to be aware of. Hydration is vital while on lithium. If your student becomes dehydrated

while taking lithium, he could suffer from lithium toxicity. There is a small range between a therapeutic level and a toxic level of lithium. If your student is on lithium he should never be denied access to water. Additionally, lithium increases the frequency of urination which means your student will need access to a bathroom.

2. **Anticonvulsants** – These are some of the same medications that are used to treat children who have seizures. These medications help to even out mood swings. Anti-convulsants frequently used to treat bipolar disorder include Lamictal, Depakote, Trileptal, and Tegretol.

3. **Antipsychotics** – The more common antipsychotic medications include Abilify, Geodon, Seroquel, Risperdal and Zyprexa. These may be used alone but are frequently used in combination therapy with either lithium or an anticonvulsant. They are known to calm aggressive-type behaviors and to stop hallucinations and psychosis but they also assist in stopping manic episodes and in some cases help with depression.

4. **Add-ons** – Depending on a specific child's medical profile and co-occurring conditions other medications may be added to address symptoms of anxiety, sleep disturbance, attention deficits, obsessions, and so on. These medications must be used carefully and with close observation because in some cases they

can cause a worsening of symptoms of bipolar disorder.

5. **Supplements** – Depending on the treating physician some children may also take supplements such as omega 3 fish oil. There are also vitamin and mineral supplements that are being studied to see if they are effective in treating children with bipolar disorder. You should however be aware that some over-the-counter supplements can worsen a child's symptoms. St. John's Wort, Valerium, and even some of the herbs found in health drinks can contribute to worsened mood swings in children with bipolar disorder.

Medications may need to be administered at school or may be given only at home. As with medication trials for other illnesses, the usefulness of any particular medication is weighed against its effectiveness versus its side effects. If your student is stopping or starting a new medication, you will want to be aware of any negative effects. Occasionally medications will cause symptoms to worsen instead of improve. Medication trials may call for extra stress reductions and understanding.

Therapy

Therapy for bipolar disorder generally involves teaching a child to recognize and monitor mood states, deal with strong emotions, develop positive coping skills, stay medication compliant and deal with the inevitable frustrations that come with the illness such as difficulty making friends or getting along with family members. This type of intervention is not enough to treat bipolar disorder on its own but in combination with medication it can help the child have longer periods of stability.

Family Support

This is another area where a teacher can have a positive impact. Raising a child with bipolar disorder can be confusing, physically exhausting, and mentally draining. Parents need all the understanding and support they can get to meet this challenge. As a teacher your willingness to learn and help make school a positive experience can go a long way to encourage and support your student's family. It's important for you to recognize that each family may be in a different stage of dealing with the illness. A family with a newly diagnosed child may be experiencing an initial stage of grief or denial and could benefit from referrals to outside sources of support and information as they begin this journey. Appendix B will give you resources you can pass on to a parent in need of support. Parents who have been dealing with a prolonged period of instability may especially appreciate your kindness and understanding as their own resources have become stretched to the limit. A family with a child who has stabilized and already has multiple supports in place may need much less.

In addition to various stages of grief, families will also vary in their level of knowledge of the illness, advocacy skills, and communications skills. Due to the hereditary nature of the illness others will be dealing with their own illness or that of a spouse or ex spouse. In all cases teamwork and good communication will be vital factors to success. Parents of children with bipolar disorder frequently deal with blame, stigma and a generally uneducated public when it comes to bipolar disorder.

This means that their first reaction may be on the defensive. Reassuring them of your support and commitment to helping their child and working together as a team may go a long way to break down those defenses and help establish a good home/school connection.

School Support

This, of course, is where you play a very large role. Without effective school support, the wellness of your student with bipolar disorder can be jeopardized. School stress can precipitate worsened symptoms and even hospitalizations in some cases. School support however should not simply fall on the shoulders of one individual teacher. It takes a whole team of educators to help this child be successful in the school setting. If your student does not yet have a network of support at school, it will be vital to start building that network. Generally this will include a school counselor, a behavioral specialist, the school nurse, and a safe person or contact. As the need arises others, such as occupational therapists, may also be involved at school. Let's move further into this subject by going to the next chapter.

Chapter Six

Help at School

School S.O.S.

For most children with bipolar disorder to be successful at school, they require extra assistance and interventions. Just as students need extra assistance and help to be successful, so, too, teachers need support and assistance to help their student with bipolar disorder. Thankfully, there are provisions to help students with disabilities in school. You are likely very familiar with these roads to assistance but you may be less familiar with how these interventions can specifically be of assistance to students with bipolar disorder. One of the first steps is to get the ball rolling. While sometimes students come to you with numerous supports in place, others may be very new on this journey and not have adequate support. Don't wait until a crisis to raise a red flag that your student needs more support. The Child Find law gives schools extra reason to be vigilant in identifying all their students with disabilities. As we have seen, bipolar disorder is a serious health impairment that has many effects in the classroom. Referring a child for an evaluation or speaking with his parents about your concerns may be the beginning of long-term success for your student.

Section 504

Some students with bipolar disorder are served under a Section 504 plan, at least for a period of time. Quite often this intervention becomes a stepping stone to more extensive interventions in the future. Section 504 is part of a Civil Rights law that was aimed at preventing discrimination. If a student is considered to have an impairment that substantially limits one or more major life activities – including learning – then he may qualify for protection under this law. This is where all your previous reading to understand bipolar disorder may come to the rescue of your student. Many schools have trouble identifying exactly how bipolar disorder impairs learning because they may not be familiar with all the effects of bipolar disorder. By referring back to chapters 3 and 4 you will be able to take this information with your own student in mind and document those areas related to bipolar disorder that limit learning in his specific case.

Once your student qualifies for a 504 plan there are many accommodations that can be put in place to help him be successful. Please see the chart on pages 75 and 76 for possible accommodations that can help your student.

IDEA

Not all children with bipolar disorder receive enough assistance with a 504 plan. One study took a sampling of children diagnosed with bipolar disorder and found that 80% of them received special education services through the Individuals with Disabilities Education Act. This figure may not surprise you given all the ways bipolar disorder can impact a child in the school setting. Many school districts find that children with bipolar disorder frequently qualify under the Other Health Impaired category. Simply getting through this first phase of identification and setting up the first Individual Education Plan (IEP) is a big task that can take months. But even prior to an IEP being put in place extra considerations can be provided simply by understanding the needs of your student. For instance, you don't need a legal piece of paper to tell you that a child having frequent urination due to meds needs to be allowed extra bathroom breaks. So while you wait for the process to unfold consider the information in the rest of the book and apply as much as you can now and don't be afraid to bring in that extra help. Involve the school nurse, counselor and the special education liaison and make arrangements to help this student.

Uncovering Hidden Obstacles

One of the steps to getting an IEP in place through IDEA is a complete evaluation. Evaluations must be comprehensive and cover all aspects of the suspected disability. Use your knowledge of the effects of this illness to recommend areas to evaluate that others may not be readily aware of. For instance, given the high rates of learning disabilities with bipolar disorder you may look at a child's difficulties and see that he should be evaluated for a learning disability. Given the difficulties with sensory processing, an individual student may need an occupational therapy evaluation. If there are any other areas of specific concern, voice these so that all areas may be evaluated. This saves time and uncovers areas that, if hidden, would continue to impede your student's success.

If obstacles remain hidden then you don't have the full picture and it will be much more difficult for this child to achieve success in the classroom. Examples of hidden obstacles include:

- language processing disorders
- auditory processing disorder
- sensory sensitivities
- executive dysfunction
- dyscalculia
- dysgraphia
- dyslexia
- nonverbal learning disability
- Asperger's disorder

Is it the Right Placement?

Once a complete evaluation has taken place, the team will need to decide on the appropriate placement for the student. While some children with bipolar disorder can be successful in a mainstream environment with supports, there are many who cannot succeed in this setting. Many students with bipolar disorder will need smaller classrooms with more one-on-one attention. Some will need self-contained classrooms. Some will need a one-on-one aid for assistance and still others require placement in a therapeutic program. While the law requires the least restrictive environment, some schools make the mistake of waiting too long to move the student to a more restrictive environment. Waiting too long before placing a student in a setting with more supports can have an adverse effect on his stability.

Accommodations

After the appropriate setting is determined, it will be vital to establish and implement appropriate accommodations. Here are some of the more common accommodations provided to students with bipolar disorder.

Common Difficulty	Possible Accommodations
Trouble paying attention in class due to external stimulation/noise.	• Reduced class size • Seating near the front • Use headphones to block out noise
Easily overwhelmed and frustrated. Shuts down when presented with large amounts of work.	• Present worksheets one at a time vs. large packets of work • Reduce the amount of work
Frequent mood swings which cause both slow and lethargic or loud and energetic behaviors.	• Ignore minor behaviors during mood swings • Allow student to run outside in order to expend energy • Extended time on assignments
Numerous physical complaints such as headaches, stomach aches and back aches.	• Allowed to go to the nurse when unwell • The nurse will have instructions from child's doctor for interventions: ginger ale, ibuprofen, rest, crackers, etc.

Dry mouth and increased thirst due to medication.	• Allowed to have a water bottle in class • Allowed trips to the water fountain
Medication causes frequent urination.	• Allowed to use the bathroom as needed
Significant writing disability and hand tremors from medication.	• Allowed to dictate answers to teacher • Reduced writing assignments • Receive a copy of all classroom notes • Occupational therapy for handwriting issues • Use word processor to type
Obsesses over the safety of family members.	• Allowed to call home
Difficulty with social interaction.	• Involved in a social skills group with the behavioral specialist
Behaviors such as crying in class or angry outbursts.	• Emergency card or private signal to teacher for escape from the classroom before a meltdown • Safe contact person and safe place to go

(This chart is modified from The Childhood Bipolar Disorder Answer Book from Sourcebooks, Inc. Copyright 2008, Tracy Anglada and Dr. Sheryl Hakala. Reprinted with permission.)

Practical Application

Now let's see how we can take a practical list of accommodations together with our knowledge of the illness and put it into action by using a few of the scenarios from earlier in the book. Let's look at possible accommodations that may help each student. Remember that we aren't limited to the list of accommodations – we are really only limited by our own imagination and creativity. For the purposes of this exercise we will assume that each student has been identified as a student with a disability and either has an IEP or 504 plan, as these are our primary pathways to extra help for students with bipolar disorder. We will also assume that you are touching base with the parents of your student in order to obtain additional information and to work collaboratively to find successful interventions. In some of the scenarios we will step back a bit and see how a proactive intervention can change the course of your student's school day.

- *Example: Michael drags into class with his usual tardy slip in hand. He plops down in his chair and immediately puts his head on the desk. You ask him to take out his book and follow along. He pulls out his book slowly and turns to the right page. After you finish writing the notes on the chalkboard you turn to find that Michael is now using his book as a pillow.*

Intervention: After input from the parents, the team decides that Michael will act as an office aid for first hour and switch his academic class until later in the day when he is more alert. This will give him something physically active to do to help him with wakefulness and yet won't be overly demanding. Additionally, this may help Michael with his self-esteem as he is doing an important job and receiving positive feedback. It also allows close contact with the counselor whose office is right next door.

- *Example: Emma has seemed withdrawn and emotionally delicate for the past week. She has come to your desk on several occasions with teary eyes and asked to be excused to go to the bathroom. Today she breaks down in tears for no apparent reason. Your other students are whispering and pretending not to look at her. She runs out of class and down to the counselor's office. The next day you hear that she is refusing to come to school.*

Intervention: After the second time that Emma comes to you with teary eyes asking to be excused to go to the bathroom, you implement a proactive strategy. You ask Emma to stay after class for a few minutes. Emma says she doesn't know why she is getting tearful but she is scared that she will cry in class. She seems ready to cry right now. You reassure Emma that if she needs to collect herself that you will allow her that space. Together the two of you devise a secret signal that will allow her to leave the classroom and report to Ms. Willow, who is the art teacher and her safe person. Ms. Willow has a small room off the main class where Emma can safely calm her emotions. Emma immediately experiences a feeling of relief knowing that she will not be embarrassed by her emotions in class. Emma only needs to use her safe place a few times but she knows it's there if she needs it.

- *Example: Christopher hasn't turned in a homework assignment all week. He seems listless and uninterested. You warn him that he will not be able to participate in the school rally on Friday unless he turns in all his assignments. His reply of "Whatever!" doesn't give you any hope that the work will get done.*

Intervention: On Tuesday you notice that Christopher didn't turn in his homework and you see a note in his planner from his mother that he seems to be heading toward depression. You notice that his demeanor has changed and you can see that he is getting overwhelmed with his work in class. You let him know not to worry about his previous day's assignment, giving him a fresh start. You cross out all the odd problems on his math in class and for his homework tonight you again reduce the amount of problems he has to do. He is able to successfully complete the lesser workload. All week he completes fewer problems per assignment as instructed but turns in every assignment. He gets to participate with his peers at the school rally.

- *Example: William is playing team sports during gym class. He seems to find all the dangerous spots on the court and has been knocked down several times. Now, as the team is supposed to be running laps, they stop and point at the bleachers. When you look up you see William on top of the railing of the highest bleacher attempting a dangerous high-wire act.*

Intervention: After William is knocked down, you keep a close eye on him and realize that he seems to be deliberately putting himself in harm's way. You pull William out of the game and ask him to get a drink.

After cooling down a bit, you ask William to assist the other coach with putting away the play equipment. You keep a close eye on William and keep him in goal-directed activities until the end of class. You report the incident to his classroom teacher and his parents.

- *Example: Sophia sits in your history class with a hollow, empty look. After the lecture you ask if there is anything bothering her. Sophia says, "Don't you think it's sad that all the people we are studying are dead?" As you try to explain how their accomplishments continue to live on and influence the present world, Sophia seems to have slipped back into her own private thoughts.*

Intervention: Sophia's comment lingers in your thoughts and you report it to both her parents and the behavioral specialist. Your input helps lead to a change in her medication.

- *Example: Beth has been thinking about her funeral and death. You notice that she gives a fellow classmate her calculator and she gives her necklace to another student. She seems preoccupied in class writing a note in her notebook instead of listening. She doesn't write down the assignment. The next day her seat is empty and it isn't until later that you learn she has been hospitalized after a suicide attempt.*

Intervention: After observing Beth's suspicious behavior, you ask her if everything is okay. When Beth becomes emotional you call the behavioral specialist to your classroom. The behavioral specialist accompanies Beth to her office where Beth reveals her suicide note and her plans. Beth's parents are called and Beth is admitted to the hospital for a crisis intervention and medication adjustment. While Beth is in the hospital you have the class decorate handmade cards to her telling her she is missed. Before returning to the classroom after her hospital discharge, you meet with the IEP team to see what special needs she has for the transition back to class.

- *Example: Susan is trying to work as a team with her partner Alicia but Alicia is irritable and argumentative. The two are unable to come to an agreement on even minor aspects of the project. Alicia feels that it is all Susan's fault. When you try to point out ways to work together, Alicia becomes angry with you and says that you are causing the whole problem.*

Intervention: You respond with a low, calm voice and ask Alicia if she would like to work on her own for a little bit. Alicia continues to be angry and argumentative. You maintain a nonthreatening, calm voice and ask Alicia how you can help her. Alicia says she doesn't know. She remains irritable. You ask her if she needs a break from the classroom. She says "Yes!" and reports to the counselor's office. The next day you talk with Alicia before class and ask if she would like to work on her own today. She says she is feeling better today and would like to try working on a team again. Alicia works well with her new partner today.

- *Example: Joel is supposed to complete a math sheet with 20 problems on it before lunch. Joel makes an attempt to start the problems but has to restart every few minutes after something distracts him. By lunchtime the worksheet is not even a third of the way completed.*

Intervention: You notice that Joel is becoming very distracted. You move him away from the busy part of the room into the reading corner where there are fewer distractions. You let him work with a pair of headphones on with soft music playing in the background. This seems to help him focus and he is able to complete his worksheet in time for lunch.

- *Example: Mary loudly complains when she is given her assignment. She says it's for babies and insulting. She refuses to even look at it. She interrupts your lecture and proceeds to explain why you and your way of teaching are wrong.*

Intervention: You have seen Mary become grandiose before. You refuse to engage in a power struggle or to argue with her. You know that you cannot reason with her when she is in this mood state. You see if you can redirect Mary by asking her to work on a project about this topic that she could present to the class. This makes Mary feel good and she becomes absorbed in her project for about 10 minutes but then seems to crash, putting her head on the desk and falling asleep. You let her rest as you can see she is not stable. You make sure to document her mood change on the daily mood chart for her doctor.

- *Example: Mark receives his assignment but he alternates between staring at the paper and turning his gaze to every tiny disturbance in the room. When you prompt him to begin he says he doesn't know what to do despite the fact that you just went through the instructions.*

Intervention: You go over the instructions again with Mark and ask him to repeat them back to you. Because

Mark is still having racing thoughts, he is unable to collect himself to do this independent work. You ask Mark to move to the computer and complete an alternate task which engages all of his senses.

- *Example: Ethan begins to take his timed math test. He sees ants crawling on his paper. They feel like they are crawling up his arm. Ethan pushes his paper to the floor. The teacher picks it up as the timer buzzes and writes a zero in red ink. As she puts the paper back on Ethan's desk he sees the red ink turn to blood and drip down. He wads it up and throws it away never once telling the teacher or other students what he saw.*

Intervention: You walk by Ethan's desk just as he throws his paper on the floor and the timer goes off. You kneel down by his desk and notice a strange look in his eye. You ask why he threw the paper on the floor. He doesn't answer you. You ask if he would like to dictate the answers to the class aide instead. Ethan responds in the affirmative but asks if the aide can write on a new paper. When you ask why, Ethan just shrugs. You tell him that it is fine to use a new piece of paper. Ethan seems relieved and scores 100% on his test.

Why Some Good Interventions Fail

Not all interventions are going to work for every child. Sometimes an intervention will work for a little while but then lose its effectiveness. Even very good interventions sometimes fail. When this happens it is time to reassess the intervention. The reasons for an intervention failing can be complex but understanding those reasons can help the team supporting this student to find alternate interventions that work. Here is a real-life example of a good intervention that failed:

- **Intervention** – Matthew is a middle school student with bipolar disorder and learning disabilities. He spends most of his day in smaller classrooms and receives special education instruction. One of Matthew's disabilities is an auditory processing disorder. He incorrectly processes up to one-third of the spoken word. The IEP team implemented the use of a portable FM Trainer. Matthew is to give a microphone to each of his teachers and set the amplifier on his desk. After trialing this intervention for six weeks it is noted by his teachers that Matthew is not consistently using his FM Trainer. He frequently fails to give the microphone to his teachers and essentially the intervention is not being utilized. When asked if the device helps him, Matthew confirms that it does. When asked why he doesn't use it, he says it takes too long.

- **Investigation** – The behavioral specialist called Matthew to his office to talk to him about using his FM Trainer. Matthew insisted that it took too long to use and that by the time he had it set up and ready that he missed out on the teacher's instructions to the class. The behavioral specialist was skeptical but swiveled his perspective by asking Matthew to demonstrate how he set up the FM Trainer so that he could understand why it took so long. So Matthew sat at a desk in the behavioral specialist's office and took out his book and pencil as he would for class. Then he took out his FM Trainer and placed it on his desk. He then proceeded to move his pencil and book to the other side of his desk. Next, Matthew moved the FM Trainer. Still dissatisfied with the position of the items on his desk, he moved them all again. After watching Matthew change the position of the FM Trainer, the book and the pencil for five minutes, the behavioral specialist asked him to stop and put the FM Trainer away.

- **Discovery** – The behavioral specialist later told the team what he had observed. Matthew was obsessing over the FM Trainer. He was anxious and worried that it would fall to the floor and break. He spent so much time trying to put it in the right place that the intervention itself had become a distraction and he was losing instruction time. This was an important discovery and led to the team making changes.

- **Alternate Intervention** – The IEP team determined that Matthew would no longer use the FM Trainer. Instead he would be moved to the front of the class, closer to the teacher. After the teacher gave instructions to the class she would double-check with Matthew and have him repeat the instructions to her to make sure he had processed them accurately.

Helping a student with bipolar disorder find success at school is an ongoing process riddled with challenges. His needs will change over time and so will the interventions. But there is help at school, as we have seen in this chapter. Accessing that help starts this child on the road to success in school but helping him move along that road takes more than an IEP or 504. It takes teachers who are compassionate and willing to learn, to go the extra mile, to implement the accommodations ... to swivel. With this in mind, how can you personally create a classroom that will nurture students with bipolar disorder?

Chapter Seven

Your Classroom

Get to Know Your Student

One of the best things you can do to begin making your classroom a place of success for your student with bipolar disorder is get to know your student. If your student already has an IEP in place with accommodations such as a safe place and safe person to go to when emotionally overwhelmed, then you will want to work out the details of this prior to the start of school. Check with the previous teacher to see what signal or method was used to implement this procedure and find out if it was successful. If this student experiences a lot of school anxiety then ideally you would have already met with him and his parents prior to the first day of school. While this may not be necessary for students who are stable and experience little difficulty in the school environment, it will be vital to students who are more symptomatic and have extensive interventions.

Communicate with Parents

Your student will have a better chance of being successful in your classroom if there is a positive teacher/parent relationship. This fosters open communication and gives you vital information that can assist you in helping your student. Here are a few conversation starters and questions you may want to ask parents in order to gather extra information that can help you set the stage for a successful year:

- What has been your child's best classroom experience and what made it that way? (Often you will find that best classroom experiences revolve directly around a teacher who "gets it" when it comes to an individual student.)

- Does the child have a co-occurring condition (tics, obsessive-compulsive disorder, ADHD, etc.)? If so, you may ask the parent to provide you with extra information regarding this condition.

- Does the child have any particular anxiety about school?

- Is the child experiencing any medication side effects (dry mouth, frequent urination, dizziness, stomach upset, cognitive dulling, etc.)?

- What are his specific stressors or triggers (crowds, excess noise level, etc.)?

- What helps him stay calm or focus better (breathing exercises, quiet place, seating position, etc.)?

- Does the child have a special gift or area of interest (music, art, hobbies, etc.)?

- How does this illness specifically affect him academically (difficulty concentrating, specific impairment, etc.)?

- Which accommodations really made a difference for your child last year?

The Environment Matters

As you contemplate how to help your student with bipolar disorder have a successful school year, it is important to swivel your attention to the environment that he will enter every day – your classroom. For your student to be successful in the classroom it must be a place where he feels safe. Because so many students with bipolar disorder have difficulty processing sensory stimuli, take a fresh look at your classroom from a sensory perspective. It will help to actually walk out of your room and enter it with a checklist to help you evaluate your room. Here is list to help you do just that:

Noise

- Is there one part of your room that is noisier than another?
- Is the air conditioner noisy?

- Is there a pencil sharpener for classroom use that makes noise?
- Are there one or two students who perpetually tap their pencils?
- Is there a different hour that has a quieter group of children (higher grades)?

Interventions: Seat your student with bipolar disorder away from the noisier areas of the room. If this does not block enough noise try a desk carrel or noise-canceling headphones. If the class that he is in is particularly noisy try rearranging his schedule so that he is part of a quieter group. Set aside five minutes in the beginning of class for all pencil sharpening to be done or provide sharpened pencils in exchange for dull ones.

Lighting

- Does your room have overhead fluorescent lighting?
- Does the sun shine brightly through the windows in a particular area?
- Do you use an overhead projector that is bright to look at?

Interventions: Make one area of your classroom a calming area by turning off the fluorescent lighting in that portion and using indirect lighting such as a lamp. Allow students with strong sensitivities to wear a visor or tinted glasses. If you use an overhead projector give your student a copy of notes so that he does not have to look at the overhead projection for a lengthy period of time.

Temperature

- Are you able to control the temperature in your room?
- Does the temperature fluctuate?
- Is one area of the room warmer/colder than another?

Interventions: Children with bipolar disorder have a difficult time regulating their internal temperatures. Keeping the temperature in the room as consistent as possible and encouraging your student to dress in layers can help.

Odors

- Do you or your students wear strong cologne or perfume?
- Is there a musty odor in the classroom?
- Is there a cleaner used in the classroom that leaves a strong smell behind?
- Do you use air fresheners?

Interventions: If the room has a musty smell ask to have the carpets cleaned. Wear minimal perfume/cologne if any at all. Use air neutralizers to remove odors instead of air fresheners, which may leave a scent behind. Try switching to milder smelling cleaners if possible.

Routine and Structure

In addition to creating an environment that doesn't assault the senses of a student with bipolar disorder, it is also helpful to create a framework of structure and routine. Students with bipolar disorder may have difficulty transitioning or shifting their attention from one task to the next. They may frequently "perseverate" or get "stuck" on an idea or on a task. This can be more pronounced when the student is having symptoms of hallucinations or other psychosis. The more their thinking becomes disorganized, the more they latch onto specific ideas or routines. Children with bipolar disorder are often black and white rigid thinkers who need a lot of structure. Having things in order and being able to rely on routine is very important for these students especially since their own inner emotions can be full of turmoil and constant change. This structure and routine becomes a familiar comfort to them.

Even the most structured classroom will have changes in schedule at times due to circumstances out of the teacher's control. Changes in schedule can also be due to field trips, assemblies, fun days, unavoidable teacher absence or statewide testing. When changes to the routine are known in advance, it may help to prep your student with bipolar disorder by giving him verbal cues about the change. Don't wait until a bell or announcement surprises the student with this change. Even when shifting attention sets means getting to do a fun activity it could still lead to an emotional meltdown. For students who change classes frequently it may be helpful to give them a 10-minute warning daily so that they can make the transition smoothly.

- *"Isaac, even though we are in the middle of math right now, we are going to have a special assembly in about 15 minutes. I know you like to get all your math problems finished so today you only need to do problems 1-5. You can be excused from the rest of the paper."* (Without this warning some students with bipolar disorder will be so hyper-focused on the problems that they should have finished that they may be unable to smoothly move into the next activity.)

In some cases it is advisable to tell him far in advance and have him write it down in his planner. This is where getting to know your student will be helpful because in other cases knowing too far in advance may simply cause undue anxiety as the student obsesses and worries over the change.

If a substitute teacher takes the reigns for a day, she should be advised of any emergency signals that you have established with this student and the student will need reassurance that these plans are still in place.

- *"Jenny, next Thursday I will be gone to a teacher workshop and Ms. Bartlett will be substituting for me that day. You remember that Ms. Bartlett substituted last month and she already knows all about our secret signal. I'm going to make a note in your planner for Thursday so you remember. If you have any trouble with your work while I'm gone you can always ask Ms. Aide for help."*

While not every change can be anticipated, you can prepare in advance for the unanticipated change in routine by developing a habitual or routine statement that cues your student into shifting attention sets. For instance, you can help your student use imagery to imagine himself putting away one task to start on another. If you are consistent with the same imagery then its use will signal the change for your student. If a student can't think in abstracts then you may have a physical task that signals the shift.

- *You are in the middle of a spelling test when an unannounced fire drill takes place. You must quickly abandon the spelling test and safely move your students along the fire escape route and out of the building. You give your students instructions and everyone starts to line up. You notice however that Ben is still in his seat. When you ask him to quickly get in line, he looks distressed and says he can't go until he finishes his test. At this point, you use the imagery that you have already established with Ben: "This test is important and we will finish it; but right now I need you to put it on a shelf. When we get back, we will take it off the shelf and start again."*

It would have been better to give your student advance notice as this would have helped to reduce anxiety and stress associated with the fire drill. But if you find yourself in an unexpected situation and need to help your student shift attention then imagery may be of assistance. Being able to mentally picture the test being put away for later may help your student detach and shift attention, or you may want to use a literal shelf where tasks are put when they have to be left for another activity.

Low Expressed Emotion

An important skill you will want to use while working with students who have bipolar disorder is low expressed emotion. This involves speaking in a calm, low, steady voice, using nonthreatening, reassuring body movements and being nonreactive when you see that your student is on the edge with his emotions. We've already seen that students with bipolar disorder may incorrectly process emotional meaning of speech. In addition, we noted that their brains are overactive in the areas of their temporal lobes instead of their frontal lobes. So instead of using logic to interpret situations, they are using the part of their brain that identifies danger and is emotionally reactive. Understanding this helps you to realize that you can't throw fuel on the fire. Raising your voice, coming toward the child in a gesture of authority or putting your hands on the child in an emotional situation are all fuel for an emotional meltdown. This will not help to subdue the child but may make him panic, run or become more oppositional, much like a cornered animal in danger.

If your student is about to lose emotional control, your goal becomes helping him maintain control. Why should this be your problem? It is for several reasons. If your student loses emotional control while in the classroom, then you lose instruction time not only with this student but with the whole class. No learning can take place in an emotionally charged situation. You also lose any rapport that you have built up with this student if a situation deteriorates. Helping him be successful in maintaining emotional control is part of helping him be successful in your classroom.

Using low expressed emotion before a situation gets out of hand can help your student settle back down into the classroom routine. Also take note if there were any triggers to the heightened emotion. Many times the trigger will pertain to an area of known difficulty such as handwriting tasks or another area of learning that is impaired. Additionally, if the student is supposed to be getting accommodations and these are not being implemented, his sense of injustice can be quite strong. Many times these students are very insightful into their own needs but may express these needs in an overreactive way. Discard the emotion but listen to what he is telling you. Then, when he is calm, come up with collaborative solutions that can avoid future outbursts altogether.

Let's consider an example. The class is given an assignment to copy notes from an overhead projector. Lori, a student with bipolar disorder and learning disabilities, has IEP accommodations for reduced handwriting. Lori is agitated and vocal about the work saying she doesn't learn this way and can't do the work. She is speaking loudly and her face is turning bright red. Let's see how two different teachers may perceive and handle the situation differently and the results.

> **Teacher A:** *Ms. Adler immediately sees Lori as a disruptive problem student. She feels that if she doesn't push Lori to do her work then she will merely skate by and never reach her full potential. Ms. Adler raises her voice and uses a sharp tone to tell Lori that if she doesn't do her work she will get detention. This agitates Lori further. She shoves her books off the desk and says the class is stupid. Ms. Adler now feels that if she doesn't react strongly and decisively that Lori will never respect her authority. She marches over to Lori and demands that she leave the room. When Lori refuses, Ms. Adler leans over her desk and loudly repeats the demand. Lori responds with a barrage of obscenities and storms out of the room. All learning for Lori has ended. All rapport between teacher and student has been lost. Lori continues to have difficulty in this class all year. She rarely accomplishes her work and is often triggered in this class finding it necessary to leave for her safe place.*

Teacher B: *Ms. Bernard has read in the IEP that Lori becomes easily overwhelmed with writing assignments. She recognizes that Lori has become frustrated and emotionally reactive. Ms. Bernard shifts into her mode of low expressed emotion. She uses a low, steady, calm voice and a short response, which is easy for Lori to process: "Okay, okay." Ms. Bernard responds as if she were soothing a hurt animal. The calm response takes Lori off guard and she is now feeling very vulnerable and on the verge of tears. Ms. Bernard continues with a soothing voice: "Let's figure something out together. Do you want to talk about this in the hall?" Lori responds in the negative because she hasn't had time to think through this new possibility. Ms. Bernard simply says, "Don't worry about the writing right now. Let's talk when you're ready, okay?" Lori gets up and goes into the hall. Ms. Bernard follows her. This is the beginning of a very good relationship between Lori and Ms. Bernard. Lori now feels comfortable with Ms. Bernard and she does some of her best work in this class. Ms. Bernard's room becomes one of her "safe" places to go when feeling overwhelmed in other classes.*

As you can see, low expressed emotion can help a student with bipolar disorder regain control. It can also help you maintain control of your own emotions when confronted with an emotional student. It leads to solutions that can help your student have success.

Facial Expression

We previously noted that children with bipolar disorder incorrectly process facial expressions. Neutral faces can be perceived as hostile. How does this information help you make your classroom environment a warm and inviting place to a student with bipolar disorder? Does this mean that you must walk around with a smile plastered on your face? That, of course, is neither feasible nor desirable. But sincere warm expression will help this student. If you are a teacher who naturally has a stern or serious expression, you may find that your student frequently thinks that you are angry with him. Just having this information will help you to understand if your student is reacting negatively to you. It may simply be that his brain is drawing the wrong conclusions and he is responding accordingly. You can help to counteract some of this effect by making it a habit to verbally express your satisfaction with the student and his work instead of simply relying on a nod or facial expression alone to convey this message. You may also find it necessary to reassure your student that you are not angry or upset. If you find that one particular student frequently thinks that you are mad with him you may want to actually address this with him. You can say something to this effect: "I know you sometimes think I'm mad at you, but I'm not. That is just the expression I have on my face when I'm teaching something really important or sometimes when I'm thinking about something totally different, like lunch!" This of course won't instantly change how he perceives your emotion but it does at least give him new information to add to the equation.

Finally, this information can be used during placement decisions. There are simply some teachers whose demeanor and expression would not be conducive to a successful environment for a student with this type of faulty processing. Assigning the student to an alternate classroom can avoid some of these misunderstandings. This knowledge may also change who you chose to seat this student next to. Just as the student may misinterpret the facial expression of a teacher, he may have a similar problem with other classmates.

Flexibility Needed

Another aspect of creating a classroom in which this student can thrive is remaining flexible. This may seem to contradict the earlier information about the need for routine and structure. Flexibility, however, can actually work quite nicely within the framework of structure and routine. Flexibility is an important part of the equation due to the nature of bipolar disorder itself. One day your student may be *on* and everything flows smoothly. The next day he may be *off* and need a great deal of assistance or simply to be left alone for a period. This variation in functioning should be anticipated. Don't fall into the trap of assuming that since the student accomplished something one day that he should be able to do the same thing on any given day.

There may also be times when your student is especially vulnerable such as right after a hospital release or during times when the student is more symptomatic. These times require a great deal of flexibility and stress reduction on your part. You may need to excuse some work, reduce work, stop homework for a while, and so on. Without such interventions, your student may end up cycling more, having a longer period of instability, back in the hospital or worse. By removing stress and being flexible, you give your student time to recover and become more stable. It is only after the child has moved toward a greater degree of stability that you can slowly start adding in additional work. At the time, you may feel rushed to get your student back up to speed but allowing your student this time to stabilize will actually contribute to his overall functioning in school.

For some students periods of instability are lengthy, which can be frustrating to both parents and teachers who would like to see him progressing in the same fashion as his peers. Sometimes entire years of progress are lost due to instability. The good news is that many children with bipolar disorder will make good leaps of progress once they stabilize and are in the correct environment. Even so, educators should not equate stability with the idea that there will be no effects from the illness.

The chart at the end of this chapter will help you see how your student's level of mood stability alters his needs in your classroom. While examining this chart, please keep in mind that it refers to levels of stability based on active symptoms. As we learned in Chapter 4, active symptoms are just one of the four ways that bipolar disorder affects the child in the classroom, so other accommodations based on the other three needs may stay constant during all these levels of stability.

A Safe Haven

With knowledge, compassion and effort you can make your classroom a safe haven for your student with bipolar disorder. The result is far from one-sided. You will be rewarded in ways you could never anticipate. You will have the pleasure of knowing this student on a new level. You will see his positive qualities and know that you are becoming an important part of his history. Perhaps he will never know everything you have done to help him but he will know that you cared. You will have the satisfaction of truly making a difference.

Level of Stability	Concern	Goal	Flexibility in School
Severely ill	Completely unstable - concerned for the safety and well-being of your student or others.	1) Maintain safety. All other concerns are inconsequential. No other learning goals can be achieved without basic safety.	May need to be on homebound instruction or in a therapeutic environment.
Critically ill	Recuperating from severe illness or is very fragile with frequent and severe mood swings. He does not function well in the outside world or at home.	1) Prevent further deterioration of health. 2) Promote recuperaion. 3) Maintain a safe environment.	May need partial school day. Will need low stress levels, low workload and no homework.
Moderately ill	Frequent mood swings but is functioning to some degree in the outside world or at home. The student may do well in one environment and not another.	1) Gradually help student build on his functioning. 2) Learn to identify mood states and triggers.	May be able to attend all day with multiple supports in place. Maintain low stress, reduce work load and reduce homework.
Mildly ill/ Partially stable	Minor mood instability but is functioning fairly well both in the outside world and at home. Stress may still induce an exaggerated response but he recuperates quickly and is able to resume activities.	1) Identify areas that could solidify your student's stability. 2) Help student learn skills that could not be mastered during instability.	Should be able to attend most days with multiple supports in place. Student may be able to handle more work but be careful not to overload. Identifying additional challenges such as learning disabilities may help the child move toward wellness.
Wellness/ Stability	Your student is mood stable and currently functioning well in the outside world and at home.	1) Optimize the length of this period of stability. 2) Monitor for early warning signs of setbacks. 3) Strengthen areas of weakness. 4) Understand any limitations that result from the illness.	Should be able to attend school with support. May be able to handle more work. Will still have unavoidable effects that should be taken into consideration. Backup plans should be in place in case of destabilization.

Chapter Eight

Tough Questions

Tackling the Tough Topics

I hope that the first seven chapters of this book have helped you understand more about students with bipolar disorder and how you can help them. As we come to the close of this book, no doubt you have a few lingering questions. Because teaching in the real world is tough, I'm going to tackle these tough questions.

1. ***What if I doubt that my student really has bipolar disorder?*** You could have doubts about a particular student's diagnosis for a variety of reasons. Diagnoses may change over time as a student develops and the full picture of his illness comes to light. While misdiagnosis does happen, keep in mind that you are only seeing a snapshot of your student's functioning. Diagnosis is made on symptoms over a period of time in varying settings. Additionally, other factors such as family history are

also considered for a diagnosis. Even if the diagnosis is later altered it may not substantially change this child's needs in the classroom. To receive the wrong diagnosis would still mean that the child was exhibiting serious symptoms of concern. If the child is later diagnosed with unipolar depression or anxiety or severe ADHD with obsessive-compulsive disorder or any number of other illnesses it is likely that he will still need very similar types and degrees of interventions to be successful. It is also possible that you may have a student diagnosed with another condition who is later reclassified as bipolar disorder. Instead of focusing on the diagnosis, focus on which interventions are effective in helping the student be successful in your classroom. You can also give the parents feedback and reporting as to what you see in the classroom which may help in the student eventually being given the correct diagnosis.

2. **What if I am trying really hard to help my student but things are going wrong?** This is frustrating to be sure – both to you and to your student. Perhaps you have tried every suggestion in this book and then some and your student is just not finding success in your classroom. Some at this point are tempted to blame the child or the parents. The problem with placing blame is it doesn't solve anything; it simply gives us permission to wash our hands of the matter. In this case, it is quite possible that neither you nor your student is to blame. It may be that the setting itself needs to be altered. The student may need a more restrictive environment with more supports in order to

succeed. Or it could be that an additional underlying problem such as a medical condition or additional learning disability has yet to be identified and this is preventing the student from being successful. Brainstorming with the IEP team to come up with additional ways to help this student may be in order.

3. *What if I know that my student needs more assistance but other school personnel are making it difficult?* I'm sure you didn't enter the teaching profession with the thought that it would be easy but that doesn't mean that you won't get frustrated when things are difficult either. Helping students with special needs will always be challenging whether that challenge comes from a situation, from parents, from school personnel or from your own feelings. One of the best ways to overcome school personnel who are blocking the road to success is to do what you do best – educate. Sometimes decisions are made out of lack of understanding, so share what you know. Another good approach is to document everything so that you can clearly demonstrate need. A final approach is to make sure that parents are pointed in the right direction. It may be that the parents are really in need of an educational advocate in order to become familiar with their rights.

4. *What if I feel that a student is using his illness as an excuse?* Bipolar disorder is sometimes called a hidden illness because others don't always recognize its full impact and limiting nature. They may be unaware of its effects on learning, executive functioning, sensory processing, social interactions,

energy levels and moods. You have spent some time reading this book and learning about these limiting factors and this may have changed your perspective about a particular student. Teachers must understand the illness and the needs of their students. At the same time, teachers must be careful not to unwittingly give students the idea that their illness makes them incapable. Students with any disability face a similar issue. It is important to teach your student that he is just as capable as the next person to achieve his goals even though his route to achieving these may differ from the next person. Think of a student in a wheelchair. He can't enter the school building the same way as a nondisabled peer. He has to use his wheelchair and perhaps travel to another side of the building where there is an entrance ramp. Can he still go in the building? Yes. We would not expect him to stand up and walk in, but neither would we expect him to simply give up. He must recognize his limitations while using appropriate compensations to reach his destination even though this may take more time and effort. The same is true of you and your student. You both must recognize limitations but at the same time use alternate paths to reach your final goals. Give your student the tools and skills he needs to be successful, but never give him reason to think that he won't achieve great things.

5. *What if the student seems fine at school but is having trouble only at home?* This can happen when the child has reached a moderate level of stability but is not yet stable. Children with less stability will not be able to keep it together for the

entire school day and children with more stability will be able to maintain better control across both environments. A child who has not yet reached that level of stability may be able to muster all of his emotional resources available to keep it together during school hours but then totally decompress as soon as he walks into the safety of his home. It should be realized that the school day is still having an impact on the child's functioning. Easing up on pressures at school and removing the stress of homework may allow a more evenly distributed mood state so that the child won't totally crash after he gets home. It also gives the student an opportunity to achieve a greater degree of wellness. The opposite scenario can actually happen as well. The student may struggle all day but then be fine in the safety of his home environment where there is less pressure. Interestingly, some people think that if a child is able to exert any control over his emotions then he could control them in every setting if he simply tried hard enough. That is incorrect thinking. Children with bipolar disorder may spend much more emotional effort than any other student in the classroom in order to maintain whatever control they can over their ever-changing emotions.

6. **What if I am just tired of dealing with my student?** If this is how you feel then you have probably reached the point of burnout. Many parents have felt a similar frustration, especially during long periods of instability. Let's be honest. Students with bipolar disorder can be some of the most emotionally taxing students. Recognizing that

you are becoming fatigued with the student is the first step to overcoming this issue. It may be that you need to recharge your own batteries in order to continue dealing with a particular student or you may need more support. Connect with other teachers who have challenging students and who can recognize your plight. They may be able to give you tips to combat your frustrations. Also, take care of the basics. Make sure you are getting enough rest, drinking enough water and maintaining your nourishment both physically and spiritually. You need all this to be able to start each new day. If, however, you find that this is a continuous problem with several students then you may need to look into moving into a different teaching role – one that is less intensive.

7. **What if I feel that my student is using manipulation to get his way?** Nobody likes to feel that he has been used or manipulated. Even the word "manipulation" has a very negative connotation. But consider for a moment what it really means. One dictionary defines *manipulation* as "skillful or artful management." Children with bipolar disorder must learn to skillfully or artfully manage both their illness and the environment around them. Such skillful management is an important coping skill for future success. So if your student is manipulating circumstances don't immediately conclude that this is a bad thing. However, if your student is using methods that are harmful or inconsiderate of others then you will want to help him come up with a positive coping skill to replace the harmful one.

8. *What if I feel my student is overmedicated or on the wrong medication?* Your feedback is very important. Be sure to report to parents if your student is overly sedated or experiencing numerous medication side effects in the classroom. There may be reasons that a student will have to stay on medications even when he is having some obviously negative effects. For instance, if a student is having hallucinations he may have to take a larger dose of a medication which causes him to be quite sedated. Once the hallucinations are stopped the medication may be changed or the dose lowered. It can be hard for an outside observer to understand why a medication with a strong side effect would be tolerated but when the alternate choice is worse for the child then this may be a necessity, at least for a time.

9. *What if my student is disturbing others in the classroom?* As a teacher, you are concerned with your entire classroom community. When one student disturbs learning for others this is a problem. At the same time, the classroom as a whole can also learn that there are special needs within all communities. Empathy and compassion for others with these needs can be an important life lesson. Seating your student with bipolar disorder near you is a good step to minimize distractions to others in the class. Frequent redirections may be needed. Also, keeping your student with bipolar disorder engaged can limit the distractions to others. Giving the student a busy task such as wiping the chalkboard or running an errand can

help him feel needed and keep him busy so that he is not distracting others in the class. If your student needs to move and get out of the classroom this can be accomplished through something as simple as writing a note to another teacher and sending your student to deliver it. The contents of the note are irrelevant as it is the trip out of the classroom that is important. This can all take place with minimal disruption to the classroom.

10. What if I have a student who has "rages"?
People define rages in different ways but generally these involve a prolonged period of loss of control. A student in a rage may become physically aggressive to either people or property. Not all children with bipolar disorder have rages and children with other conditions can also have rages. The latest study on children who were hospitalized after a rage indicates that these children typically need highly structured and low stress environments in order to function. Rages were also highly correlated to language processing disorders. Because of this correlation it would be good to have this child evaluated for a language processing disorder. An additional evaluation by an occupational therapist for sensory sensitivities may also be in order. Practicing low expressed emotion as discussed earlier can help to diffuse a situation before it explodes. Additionally, it should be noted that a child who is prone to rages may experience a strong degree of tactile defensiveness. This means that any touch during a period when the child has his senses heightened may be perceived as threatening and may overwhelm the student further

causing more agitation. So while you may feel that you are trying to calm the child by touching his arm or back, this may actually escalate the situation. It will be important for this child to be in the correct setting and to have a functional behavioral assessment and behavior intervention plan in place. This will help to identify if there are any triggers that precipitate the episode and will outline exactly what should be done if behaviors start to escalate prior to a full-blown rage. There should be a place of safety designated ahead of time for a child who is prone to meltdown. This keeps others in your classroom safe and allows the student to collect himself away from the eyes of others.

11. **What if my student with bipolar disorder is missing an excessive amount of school days?** Missing an excessive number of school days may be a sign that the student is depressed or experiencing increased anxiety or instability. Missing days may simply be unavoidable for a time. All but essential work may need to be excused. Your student may benefit from half-days for a period or even homebound instruction if necessary. Learning sometimes must take a backseat when the health of the student is at risk.

12. **What can I do to help my student feel like he fits in?** Fostering an environment of acceptance can go a long way to helping your student fit in. Arranging buddies or having the counselor work with him in a social skills group can also be of help. Giving your student meaningful jobs to assist in the classroom gives him a sense of pride and purpose.

Recognizing him for his strengths and praising him in front of others will help others recognize his good qualities. Also, be careful about using social pressure on this child. While some classrooms use social pressure to help students conform to classroom rules, this is a fast way to make other students in the class feel very negatively about a student with bipolar disorder. This can further his sense of isolation.

13. **What if my student expresses a suicidal thought?** If your student expresses a suicidal thought it is vital that you listen and act. His parents should be notified immediately and a counselor or behavioral specialist should consult with the child. It is not your call to decide if the child is making a serious threat. Too much is at stake. You should also avoid making the student feel guilty about expressing himself. Being able to tell an adult is very important for children who are thinking about suicide.

14. **What if my student wants to call home?** Schools and families address this request in different ways. Some students with bipolar disorder obsess over the safety of family members. Others suffer from separation anxiety. If calling home helps your student to stay in the classroom versus leaving school then it may be an acceptable request. It may also calm an anxious child or keep a child from melting down. On the other hand a call home may make matters worse for some children if they hyper-focus on wanting to leave. Discuss with

parents and the IEP team how calls home will be handled.

15. **What if my student is constantly at the nurse's office missing instruction?** If a student is frequently leaving the room to go to the nurse, it may be a sign of overall instability but it could also be a sign that something is overwhelming the child in the classroom. Note when the child is leaving and see if you find a pattern. A functional behavior assessment may identify something that precipitates the need to leave the classroom. Also, be sure to use the checklist regarding possible sensory issues (Chapter 7) that could be affecting the child in the classroom. A brief trip to the nurse may be a necessary break for a student with bipolar disorder. If you want to avoid the trip to the nurse then you may want to arrange to have a break area in the classroom itself. Some teachers keep a snack and drink in the room for their students. This can make a big difference in helping them get through the day.

16. **What if other students want to know more about bipolar disorder?** Classmates may be curious about bipolar disorder. Check with your student and his family to see if they are comfortable sharing information. Some are quite open and want the class to learn about bipolar disorder. Others will be more private regarding the diagnosis. If a family is open to the idea, you can use age appropriate materials to help others in the class learn about bipolar disorder. Some states now include mental health in their state goals for health education. If this is the case in your state, then health class may

be a vehicle to discuss such conditions as bipolar disorder. For ideas on age appropriate information visit: www.bpchildren.org.

17. **What if I suspect a student has bipolar disorder but is undiagnosed?** This student may or may not have bipolar disorder but you are not in a position to diagnose. You can, however, report to parents areas of concern and let them know what you see in the classroom. Using what you know can help any students with mood swings whether they have an official diagnosis or not.

18. **What if a parent refuses to treat a student with bipolar disorder?** Some parents refuse to take their child for treatment. Others have had very negative treatment experiences and have withdrawn their child from treatment. Still others pursue alternative treatment methods. You will not always agree with the path that parents chose for their children but you can continue to guide and support your student during the time he is with you in the classroom. It may also be beneficial to report any behaviors of concern to parents and the school's behavioral specialist and social worker.

19. **What if the other teachers involved with this student don't understand bipolar disorder?** It can be frustrating when you are working very hard to help a student with bipolar disorder only to see that progress knocked down when the student leaves your class for another where the teacher is not on the same page. This is the same world parents have been dealing with for years. Lack of

understanding abounds and so does lack of willingness to learn. At the same time the majority of teachers are very caring individuals who want to help their students succeed, they just may not know how. You may be able to help your student outside of your own classroom in several ways. You can become a contact person and safe place for this student. You can also share information with other teachers working with the student. Such information presented from a colleague may be more palatable to a reluctant teacher than if it is presented by parents.

20. **What if my student is hospitalized?**
Hospitalizations can be a very good thing if it leads to stabilization or better treatment. At the same time hospitalizations are very difficult and traumatic times for families of children with bipolar disorder. A thoughtful note and caring inquiry about the well-being of the family may be very much appreciated. Some families feel as if they are treated like lepers when a child enters a psychiatric hospital. Children who are hospitalized for other illnesses often get cards from classmates, especially in elementary school. This would be a nice gesture for your student with bipolar disorder as well. Additionally, you will want to think about the transitioning when this student returns. Full recovery after a hospitalization can take many months. Your student may be fragile for a period of time and require extra interventions and more stress reduction. Arranging this in advance will avoid overwhelming your student when he returns.

More Information

If you would like more information on childhood bipolar disorder please visit www.bpchildren.org. Be sure to visit our page just for teachers and check out these books:

The Childhood Bipolar Disorder Answer Book: Practical Answers to the Top 300 Questions Parents Ask

Intense Minds: Through the Eyes of Young People with Bipolar Disorder

Brandon and the Bipolar Bear: A Story for Young People with Bipolar Disorder

Turbo Max: A Story for Friends and Siblings with Bipolar Disorder

Imagine That ...

You drive onto campus happy that you are really headed to the presentation by your hero and not just dreaming. When you enter the lecture hall you see that there is no line to register but there are name tags and Sharpies on a table. You walk over and pick up a name tag, turning it over in your hand while you remember your dream. The woman at the table hands you a Sharpie. What will you write? Before your dream last night, you wouldn't have given this a second thought. Your name would have been scrawled quickly on the name tag and you would have been off. But today you take a moment to be grateful that no one is judging you by your worst trait. Then, with a quick flash of the Sharpie, you draw a smiley face on your name tag and enter the main auditorium with a bounce in your step. Suddenly you have the feeling that it's going to be a good night ... a very good night. It's the night you receive the Silver Apple award in recognition of your work with special needs students.

The presenter, your hero, walks to the podium. He steps up on the stool at the base of the podium, which enables his small frame to see over the top. As your 10-year-old student with bipolar disorder faces his fear of social settings to give his speech, your eyes fill with tears of pride. He concludes his speech very simply ...

"I don't know what I'd do without you.
Thank you for being my teacher
And thank you for caring!"

Appendix A

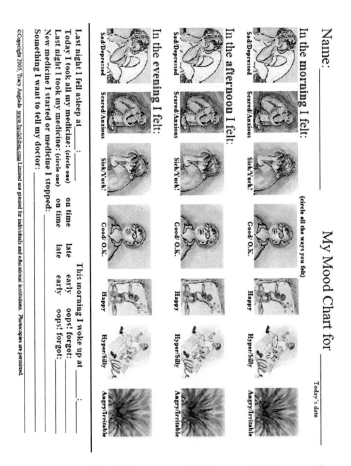

Links to a printable copy of this mood chart and a girl's version of this chart may be found at:
http://www.bpchildren.org/Charting.html
Please feel free to use these with your students.

Appendix B

BPChildren
P.O. Box 380075
Murdock, FL 33938
www.bpchildren.org

The Child & Adolescent Bipolar Foundation
820 Davis St., Ste. 520
Evanston, IL 60201
847-492-8519 Phone
847-492-8520 Fax
Web: www.bpkids.org

Depressive and Bipolar Support Alliance
730 N Franklin St., Suite 501
Chicago, IL 60610-7224
Phone: 800-826-3632
Web: www.dbsalliance.org

Federation of Families for
Children's Mental Health
9605 Medical Center Dr., Suite 280
Rockville, MD 20850
Phone: 240-403-1901
Web: www.ffcmh.org

International Society for Bipolar Disorders
P.O. Box 7168
Pittsburgh, PA 15213-0168
Phone: 412-605-1412
Web: www.isbd.org

Juvenile Bipolar Research Foundation
550 Ridgewood Rd.
Maplewood, NJ 07040
Phone: 866-333-JBRF
Web: www.jbrf.org

The National Alliance on Mental Illness
3803 N. Fairfax Dr., Ste. 100
Arlington, VA 22203
Phone: 888-999-6264
Web: www.nami.org

National Institute of Mental Health
6001 Executive Blvd., Room 8184, MSC 9663
Bethesda, MD 20892-9663
Phone: 866-615-6464
Web: www.nimh.nih.gov

National Mental Health Association
2001 N Beauregard St., 12th Floor
Alexandria, VA 22311
Phone: 800-969-NMHA
Web: www.nmha.org

STARFISH Advocacy Association
3341 Warrensville Center Rd.
Shaker Heights, OH 44122
Web: www.starfishadvocacy.org

Appendix C:
My School Day without Help

I struggle to open my eyes. Leave me alone. I want to sleep. My body is heavy, my head is swirling. How long has my alarm been ringing? Okay, I'm awake. I sit up in bed dazed. "Hurry, Hurry or you'll be late! Why are you so sleepy?" My nightmare woke me up. I couldn't sleep, I needed to stay awake. I didn't want to dream again. I stumble to my dresser. Where are the socks I like? Not this pair! They never feel right. The top is crooked and they go up too high. I hate the way they feel! No choice. On to breakfast. Who ate my waffles? There is only one left. You know I need two. One is uneven. I NEED two. There aren't two. I won't eat. I'll just brush my teeth. I can't go in the bathroom. It was in my nightmare. The bathroom isn't safe. I can't brush my teeth. It's time to leave. I can't leave. What if my house catches on fire? What if my parents die? I need to stay home. My stomach is churning. I feel sick. Can't I stay home?

The hall is noisy. Kids are pushing. Don't touch me! My sock is crooked. It bothers me. I'm so hungry. First hour I fall asleep on my desk. The kids laugh when the teacher wakes me up to go to the next class. Am I dreaming again? Is this real? I watch all the kids in class. It's like watching a play. Are they laughing at me again? What are they happy about? It's so hard to smile. Which hour am I in? What is my next class? When does it start? I don't remember. Why can't I remember? What if I go to the wrong class? I better check my schedule.

"Don't fidget in class. Pay Attention! You can check your schedule later." I don't listen. I have to know what comes next. Okay...third hour is next. I won't go to the wrong class. Extra work because I didn't pay attention? Not again!!

Third hour is test time. I can't concentrate when my sock bothers me. Is my mom okay? I need to call her. I know they won't let me call unless I'm sick. My stomach is rumbling. Can I go to the nurse? Okay, I'll finish my test tomorrow. I call from the nurse's office. Nobody answers. Mom didn't say she was going somewhere today. Did the house catch on fire? Is she okay? My stomach churns. The nurse gives me crackers to settle my stomach. That helps. Go back to class. Finally it's lunch time. What is that smell??!! I hate the way the lunch room smells. It's so loud in here. I have one friend. He's absent today. Where will I sit? I find a place in the corner of the room and eat. I hope nobody notices me.

P.E. is next. I love P.E. I run and jump, my body is light and fast now. I'm awake. I'm the BEST basketball player! I can make every shot. Why should I pass you the ball? Sit on the bench? But it wasn't my fault, he was in the way. He shouldn't take the ball from me. That makes me SO MAD! I'm HOT and my sock isn't right! I could redesign this gym. The bleachers don't belong here. Is my mom okay? I remember my dream. I don't want to remember my dream. I have to move or I will die. I run up and down the stairs.

Fifth hour is science. I feel better. Mr. Science is cool. He knows me. He knows I'm smart. I get to do experiments. It keeps my mind busy. He sends me to the office to run an errand. I'm important to him. Maybe the office lady will let me check on my mom.

She asks me why I need to call. I can't tell her. It will sound stupid. I tell her I don't remember if I am supposed to ride the bus or be picked up. She believes me. Please answer!

"Mom, are you picking me up today?"

"Of course, I am. I told you that this morning. Is everything okay?"

"Yeah, bye!"

Relief! She's okay. Back to science. Only one more class left. I can make it now. Last hour. I sit through math. The teacher is glaring at me. Am I supposed to be doing something? It's my homework. Where is it? I did it. I can't find it in my bag. "Do you want to fail?" She yells at me! I feel stupid. I know I did it. I just can't find it. My stomach churns again. I need to get out of here. The classroom is noisy. My head will explode if I don't leave. Please let me leave. Can I use the bathroom? I really have to go! I walk as slowly as I can to the bathroom. My head feels better. My stomach stops churning. I reach the bathroom. I remember my dream. I can't go in. I wait outside the bathroom as long as I can. I really need to go! I run in and go as fast as I can. My heart is racing, my head is pounding. I'm breathing hard. I did it! School is almost out. I'm going to make it! Hurray! I run out of the bathroom and into Ms. Strict and knock her over. Not Ms. Strict! I didn't mean to. I'm sorry. It doesn't matter. To the Dean's office. In trouble again. I almost made it this time. I'm really sorry.

I'll try again tomorrow. I really try. School is so hard. Won't somebody help me?

Appendix D:
My School Day with Help

I struggle to open my eyes. Leave me alone. I want to sleep. My body is heavy, my head is swirling. How long has my alarm been ringing? Okay, I'm awake. I sit up in bed dazed. "Hurry, Hurry or you'll be late! Why are you so sleepy?" My nightmare woke me up. I couldn't sleep, I needed to stay awake. I didn't want to dream again. I stumble to my dresser. Where are the socks I like? Not this pair! They never feel right. The top is crooked and they go up too high. I hate the way they feel! No choice. On to breakfast. Who ate my waffles? There is only one left. You know I need two. One is uneven. I NEED two. There aren't two. I won't eat. I'll just brush my teeth. I can't go in the bathroom. It was in my nightmare. The bathroom isn't safe. I can't brush my teeth. It's time to leave. I can't leave. What if my house catches on fire? What if my parents die? I need to stay home. My stomach is churning. I feel sick. Can't I stay home?

The hall is noisy. Kids are pushing. Don't touch me! My sock is crooked. It bothers me. I'm so hungry. Before first hour I check in with the nurse like I always do. I tell her my day didn't start so good. She gives me pretzels to eat. I feel better. But what if I need to call my mom? She reminds me that I can go to Mr. Counselor anytime if I get panicked about my parents. Okay. I know I can check on them if I need to. First hour I start to fall asleep on my desk. Ms. Helpful asks me if I can help her with an activity. She knows I'm a good helper. The kids are jealous because they wish they could help too. On to second hour. I watch all the kids in class. It's like watching a play. What are they happy about? It's so hard to smile. Which hour am I in? What is my next class? When does it start? I don't remember. Why can't I remember? What if I go to the wrong class? Ms. Caring could tell I was getting uncomfortable because I turned over the red card on my desk to give her a secret message. She came over right away. "I can tell you are a little distracted. We are going to work for 10 more minutes on this project and then you can use the last five minutes of class to organize yourself. You will be going to Ms. Write's class next." She winked at me and smiled. I like Ms. Caring. I work really hard for the next 10 minutes.

Third hour is test time. I can't concentrate when my sock bothers me. Is my mom okay? I need to call her. I know I can go to Mr. Counselor if I need to. My stomach starts churning. Ms. Write asks me if I want to take the test in the small quiet room with Ms. Aide. She writes the answers as I dictate them. She knows it's hard for me to think and write at the same time. I did really well. Finally it's lunch time. What is that smell??!! I hate the way the lunch room smells. It's so loud in here. My best friend is absent today. Where will I sit? Oh there's Joe. He's my study partner in social skills class. I like him. He wants me to sit with him. I eat my lunch and talk with Joe. He doesn't like the way it smells in here either!

P.E. is next. I love P.E. I run and jump, my body is light and fast now. I'm awake. I'm the BEST basketball player! I can make every shot. Why should I pass you the ball? Oh the Coach needs me. It's time for a water break? I don't want to leave the game but coach says just for a second to get some water. The water tastes so good and cold. I didn't even know I was thirsty. I take a second drink. I feel much cooler. "Remember the best players know their teammates and make them work hard too." Yeah I shouldn't have to make all the shots. It's hard work running up and down the court all hour. Coach says I'm a good player. Then just for fun I run up and down all the stairs in the gym. It's a pretty cool gym but they really should change where the bleachers go.

Fifth hour is science. It's my favorite class. Mr. Science is cool. He knows me. He knows I'm smart. I get to do experiments. It keeps my mind busy. He sends me to the office to run an errand. I'm important to him. I'm still worried about my mom. I stop in Mr. Counselor's office. He wears funny shoes but he's nice. He lets me call my mom. I hope she's okay. I hope she answers...Please answer!

"Mom, remember you're picking me up today?"

"I remember. Are you in Mr. Counselor's office? Is everything okay?"

"Yeah, bye!"

Relief! She's okay. Back to science. Only one more class left. I can't wait to be out of school. Last hour. I sit through math. The teacher reminds me that my homework is due. Where is it? I did it. I can't find it in my bag. "Don't panic, I'm sure it's in there somewhere!" She helps me look through my bag. There it is!! How did it get in my reading folder? The classroom is getting noisy. It's giving me a headache. I feel like my head will explode if I don't leave. I turn over my red card. The teacher sees that the noise is really getting to me. She sends Joe and me together on a bathroom break. We walk slowly to the bathroom. My head feels better. We reach the bathroom. I remember my dream. I don't want to go in but I really have to go. "Are you coming?" asks Joe. "Yeah in a minute." I wait outside the bathroom as long as I can. I really need to go! I run in and go as fast as I can. My heart is racing, my head is pounding. I'm breathing hard but trying not to let Joe see it. I don't want him to know I'm scared. "Look at that!" says Joe. What is it? Suddenly I forget my dream. Somebody stuffed one of the toilets full of paper towels! What a mess! Joe and I hurry out of the bathroom. We almost knocked Ms. Strict right off her feet. Good thing I wasn't running. We tell Ms. Strict about the bathroom. "Thank you boys! Will you please go get the janitor for me so we can get this mess cleaned up? I'm so glad you boys caught it when you did."

I check in with the nurse before I go home for the day. How was my day? It was pretty good but I'm glad school is out! I'll see you tomorrow.

Thanks for all the help!

Index

A

absences, 111
accommodations, 75–76, 77–83
addiction, 44, 47
ADHD, 59, 60, 89, 104
advocacy, 69
aggression, 37, 47
agitated, 24, 26, 56, 96, 111
aid, 74
alcohol, 36
Alzheimer's, 33
Amygdala, 41
anterior, 35
Anterior Cingulate Cortex, 36
anticonvulsant, 67
antipsychotic, 67
anxiety disorder, 45, 59, 60
Asperger's disorder, 60, 74
attention, 18, 28, 36, 38, 45, 58, 63, 67, 75, 92–93
auditory processing, 39, 74, 84
autism, 40, 60

B

Basal Ganglia, 45
behavior, 18, 20, 30, 31, 45, 52, 67, 75, 80, 111, 114
behavioral specialist, 70, 76, 80, 84–85, 112, 114
blame, 69, 104
brain, 18, 22, 25, 31, 33–47, 58, 95, 98
brain abnormalities, 33–47

C

chemical, 34, 36, 38
Child Find, 71
cingulate, 35
Cingulate Gyrus, 37
civil rights, 72
cognitive dysfunction, 18, 27, 49, 58
communication, 19, 44, 66, 69, 88
conduct disorder, 60
co-occurring conditions, 49, 59, 62, 67
coping, 68, 108
cortex, 35
counselor, 51, 70, 73, 78, 81, 111, 112
creatine, 39
crying, 21, 22, 50, 58, 76
cycles, 18, 57

D

depression, 18, 21–23, 51, 52, 67, 79, 104
destructive, 24, 56
diagnose, 27, 43, 103, 104, 114
distracted, 24, 54, 82
DNA fragmentation, 37

E

elated, 24, 54
emotion, 18, 19, 26, 31, 36, 37, 39, 41, 42, 68, 78, 92, 94, 96, 98, 107, 110

energy, 18, 21, 22, 23, 24, 26, 36, 50, 53, 54, 75, 106
energy drinks, 68
environment, 29, 31, 50, 61, 74, 87, 89, 91, 97, 98, 100, 104, 107, 108, 110, 111
evaluation, 72, 73, 74, 110
executive functioning, 28, 58, 74, 105
extremes, 18, 20, 26, 27

F

facial expressions, 18, 27, 36, 40, 41, 59, 97–98, 99
fire drill, 93–94
flexibility, 99, 101
FM Trainer, 84, 85
Food and Drug Administration, 66
friends, 68
Frontal Lobe, 38
frustration, 18, 28, 68, 107, 108
functional, 34, 36, 38
functional behavioral assessment, 111, 113
Fusiform Gyrus, 40

G

gender, 41
genes, 18
gifts, 29
glutamine, 36
grandiose, 24, 55, 82
gray matter, 35, 36, 37, 39, 41, 44, 46
grief, 69
gyrus, 35

H

habit, 45, 93, 98
hallucination, 31, 57, 67, 83, 92, 109
herbs, 68
hereditary, 17, 69
hero, 11, 117
Hippocampus, 41
hospitalization, 53, 70, 80, 99, 110, 115
hypersexuality, 24, 56

I

identify, 16, 20, 31, 40, 63, 71, 72, 111, 113
imaginative, 29
imagine, 11, 54, 93
impaired judgment, 36
inappropriate, 56
Individual Education Plan, 73, 86, 87
Individuals with Disabilities Education Act, 72, 73
infancy, 43
information processing, 18, 28, 36, 37, 40
irritable, 21, 23, 24, 52, 54, 58, 81

J

judgment, 13, 36, 38

L

language, 18, 27, 38, 59
language processing disorder, 74, 110
learning disabilities, 60, 73
learning disorders, 59
lighting, 90
limbic system, 42

Lithium, 66–67
lobe, 35
lobule, 35
low expressed emotion, 94

M

mainstream, 74
mania, 18, 23
manipulation, 108
manipulator, 12–13
medication, 66–67, 68, 109
memorization, 58, 63
memory, 42, 44, 58
mixed state, 26
mood, 44
motivation, 42, 44
Motor Cortex, 44
movement, 44, 45

N

N-acetylaspartate, 39
neuronal loss, 37, 39
nightmare, 13, 23, 122, 125
noise, 24, 54, 75, 88, 89, 90
normal, 19

O

obsessive compulsive
    disorder, 45, 59
occupational therapy, 73,
    110
odors, 91
oppositional defiant
    disorder, 59, 60
Orbitofrontal Cortex, 44

P

panic disorder, 59
parents, 69, 114
perseverate, 92

perspective, 15, 16, 22, 33,
    84, 89, 106
placement, 74
Prefrontal Cortex, 38, 40
Putamen, 45

R

racing thoughts, 24, 31, 83
rage, 110
responsibility, 44
Right Nucleus Accumbens,
    45
routine, 91

S

sad, 19, 21, 40, 52, 80
safety, 21, 52, 76, 107, 111,
    112
school anxiety, 87
Section 504, 72
seizures, 33, 67
self-contained classroom,
    74
sensory information, 46
sensory motor integration,
    45
sensory processing, 63, 73
sensory sensitivities, 28, 59,
    74, 110
Septum Pellucidum, 42
Shakespeare, 14
side effects, 49, 61
sleep/wake cycle, 46
social, 38, 47, 51, 59, 61,
    76, 105, 111, 112, 117
social worker, 114
spatial orientation, 46
St. John's Wort, 68
stigma, 14, 61, 63, 69
stimuli, 37, 39, 89

LaVergne, TN USA
19 November 2009
164650LV00004B/18/P